To
Jean Thompson

Acknowledgements

The authors are most grateful to the following for their help:-
Jean Thompson for many weeks spent proof reading and editing
Mr Harrison - Swan Hotel, Thornthwaite
Howard Porter, Milnthorpe
John Lagoe, Grasmere
George Bott, Keswick
Phil Williamson, Outward Bound Ullswater
Donald Angus, Threlkeld
Geoff Bland, Carlisle
Des and Margaret Oliver, St John's in the Vale
Stan Edmondson, Seathwaite
John Nicholson, Ravenglass
Mrs Iona Frost-Pennington, Muncaster Estate
The Polish Air Force Association in Great Britain
The Ministry of Defence Air Records
The National Trust, on whose land many of the monuments are to
be found. Particular thanks for access to records to Linda Bowden,
Keeper of Records at Grasmere, and Miss J.L. Harley, Senior Archi-
vist, London
The Forestry Commission
Workington Library
Whitehaven Library
Carlisle Library
County Records Office, Carlisle
County Records Office, Whitehaven
John Hayton, Loweswater
Joe and Dot Jackson, Lamplugh
H. F. Holidays
Keswick Mountain Rescue Team
Cockermouth Mountain Rescue Team
Robert Edmondson, Seatoller
The Harrison family, Brotherilkeld, Eskdale
Mrs Pam Bryden, Seaton
John Spedding Esq, Mirehouse, Keswick
Leconfield Archives, Cockermouth
The Times Obituaries
Londonderry Central Library, N. Ireland

The following publications were of particular help:-
Ruskin by Quentin Bell
Iteriad (Three weeks among the lakes) by John Ruskin, edited by
James S Dearden
Seathwaite Wad and The Mines of The Borrowdale Valley by Ian
Tyler
Tennyson - The Unquiet Heart by Robert Bernard Martin
Letters & Friendships of Cecil Spring Rice edited by Stephen Gwynn
Letters of Matthew Arnold
The National Trust, the Early Years by Merlin Waterson
Websters Biographical Dictionary
The Letters of William & Dorothy Wordsworth - arranged and
edited by Ernest de Selincourt
Who Was Who 1929-40
The Lake District & the National Trust by B. L. Thompson
The Journals of the Fell & Rock Climbing Club
Past & Present at the English Lakes and other publications by Rev.
H. D. Rawnsley
Literary Celebrities of the Lake District by F. Sessions
The Concise Dictionary of National Biography 1901-70
Book of poems by Cecil Spring Rice
Air crashes in the Lake District 1936-1976 by Michael J. Hurst
The annual reports of Keswick Mountain Rescue Team
100 Great Nineteenth Century Lives - edited by John Canning
Dictionary of National Biography 1912-1921
Who Was Who in Cumberland and Westmorland
Cumbria magazine
Whitehaven News
Cumberland Paquet
West Cumberland Times & Star

A special thanks to a member of Cockermouth Mountain Rescue Team
and Lake District National Park voluntary warden, Derek Tunstall
of Arlecdon. His knowledge of the locations of Lake District
monuments has been invaluable.

Photographs by Bob Orrell

Contents

......contents cont.

Introduction

In 1995 I was walking up Fleetwith Pike in Buttermere when I was stopped by two holiday makers who asked me if I knew the story of Fanny Mercer, remembered on a white wooden cross fixed near the foot of the crag. I had to admit I didn't, but in the process of finding out I came across many other interesting stories about the solitary cairns, crosses and plaques to be found all over the Lake District, and they were the inspiration for this book.

On the fells and in the dales there are literally hundreds of monuments in one form or another, and in researching, photographing and selecting fifty for this book, Margaret Vincent and I tramped miles over the fells and spent long hours sorting out fact from fiction.

The object of the book is to add a completely new dimension to the pleasure of walking in the Lake District or exploring the area by car, but we are conscious of the fact that, while some monuments record a joyous occasion, others commemorate a tragedy and we would wish their dignity to be respected.

The locations of the monuments vary from roadside verges to the summits of the highest fells, and for this reason we have divided them into three categories:-

A - a difficult fell walk - recommended safety equipment, strong boots, waterproof clothing, and a knowledge of navigation essential.

B - moderately difficult - boots or stout shoes and waterproof clothing advised.

C - easy - no special clothing or equipment needed.

This edition concentrates on monuments in North Lakeland, which is very roughly north of a line drawn across the Lake District above Grasmere. Monuments of South Lakeland is in preparation.

Bob Orrell

Aircraft Landing - Helvellyn

Inscription

The first aeroplane to land on a mountain
in Great Britain did so on this spot.
On December 22nd 1926
John Leeming and Bert Hinkler
In an Avro 585 Gosport landed here
and after a short stay flew back to Woodford.

O.S. Map: English Lakes NE 1:25000   **Grid ref:** 342152
Grade: A
Location
By the side of the path a few metres south of Helvellyn summit cairn.
Information
The two pilots, John Leeming, chairman of the Lancashire Aero Club and Bert Hinckley, from Manchester, had actually made an attempt to land on Helvellyn on December 21, but decided against it and flew off to Lancaster. They tried again the following day and had a very bumpy flight over the Lake District, with one heart-stopping occasion when the aircraft dropped down nearly five hundred feet in an air pocket. Over Helvellyn, however, they were able to manoeuvre with comparative ease and, after circling three

7

times in a descending spiral over the summit, they landed at 1.30 p.m. and taxied to a halt overlooking Striding Edge. Brought to a standstill facing north, the aircraft began to run backwards down the hill and Bert Hinckley had to keep the engine running on a full throttle until John Leeming could jump out and find stones to put behind the wheels.

The only witness to the historic occasion was a solitary walker, Professor E.R. Dodds of Birmingham; and, though there is no record of what he thought about this novel form of environmental pollution invading the peace of the fells, he at least signed a paper confirming that the landing had taken place. After staying for about twenty minutes taking photographs, the flyers prepared for the difficult up-hill take-off, and the Professor must have held his breath as the Avro, having slowly gathered speed, shot over the edge of the summit precipice above Red Tarn and dropped like a stone, gaining flying speed just in time to clear the jagged rim of Striding Edge. It was a near thing, but the troubles of the flyers were by no means over. The aircraft was desperately short of fuel and the pilots had to make a forced landing on the edge of Lake Windermere. An observer at the time wrote 'the machine was flying at a great height over the head of Lake Windermere, and after describing several circles, it came down, with engine missing badly, in Calgarth Park'. By an odd chance it landed in front of a children's hospital and there was great excitement among the children, who were having their Christmas party and rushed out thinking it was Father Christmas arriving with presents. The pilots must have had an embarrassing time talking their way out of that!

Hitching a lift to a nearby garage to buy a few tins of petrol, the flyers managed to re-fuel and were soon in the air again, arriving back at Woodford at 4.20 p.m.

Note: The original letters on the memorial stone were lead plugs which eventually rotted away. Des Oliver, a National Park Ranger who for many years climbed Helvellyn every day to prepare a fell-top weather report, instigated a move to replace it and Michael Berry, the owner of the Low Wood Hotel near Ambleside, offered to meet the cost. John Gaskell, a Keswick stonemason, carved the inscription on the new stone and delivered it to the site on the summit of Helvellyn tied onto his trials motorbike. The new stone was attached to the existing one.

8

Arthur Leonard Memorial - Cat Bells

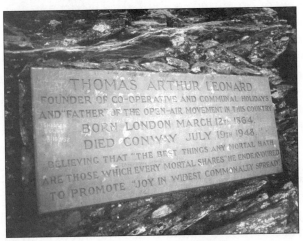

Inscription

Thomas Arthur Leonard
Founder of co-operative and communal holidays
and father of the open air movement in this country
Born London March 12th 1864
Died Conway July 19th 1948
Believing that 'the best things which any mortal hath
are those which every mortal shares' he endeavoured
to promote 'joy in widest commonality spread'.

O.S. Map: English Lakes NW 1:25000   **Grid ref:** 246210
Grade: C

Location

By the side of the path, a short distance up Cat Bells from Hawse End.

Information

T. Arthur Leonard was a Congregational Minister in the Lancashire town of Colne, and he organised group holidays to the countryside for workers from the industrial towns of the north west who wanted an alternative to the bright lights and promenades of Morecambe and Blackpool. The first holiday he organised was in June 1891, when thirty members of the Young Men's Guild stayed three nights away from Colne and walked each day on the fells around Ambleside. It was a great success and many other low-cost holidays were organised in the Lake District and North Wales, which led to Arthur Leonard founding the Christian Holidays Association, (later changed to the Countrywide Holidays Association and now called CHA Holidays.) These early holidays were very spartan and, as the demand increased, properties were sought after to open as permanent centres where comfortable accommodation could be provided for walkers in a communal environment.

In 1913 Arthur Leonard founded the Holiday Fellowship, a separate organisation but with similar principles to the CHA, and from a humble beginning has grown HF Holidays, an organisation which offers an enormous range of holidays world-wide, and which owns 19 Country House Hotel Estates throughout England, Scotland and Wales. Standards of accommodation have very much improved since the early days when Arthur Leonard led his Young Men's Guild on their first Lakeland walking holiday, but the principles on which the organisations were founded are still adhered to.

Barnard's Cairn - Ennerdale

Inscription

The Body of
Edward Barnard
of Angel St & Highbury Grove, London
who was lost in this district Augt 14th
was found on this spot
Sept 10th 1876

The builders of this cairn request
that visitors will respect its
purpose and not mark it with
initials. Octr 1876

O.S. Map: English Lakes NW 1:25000
Grade: C

Location

For years this monument was one of Ennerdale's best kept secrets and, reluctant to have the dubious honour of being the first to pinpoint its exact position, we dangle the following carrot:-

Leave the ford with back to Gabel
Down forest road through Spruce you'll travel.
But don't explore each rocky cleft
Lookingstead upon the left,
Where by the edge of roadman's pride
Sits a rock, grass topped and grey on side
And almost facing, in reedy bed
Sits another rock, but this one's red.
Face the fell then climb the side
And you'll reach the spot where Barnard died.

Information

Early on the morning of Monday, August 14, 1876, Edward Barnard, a London silversmith, waved goodbye to his wife and daughter at the Scawfell Hotel, Rosthwaite, and strode briskly up the track to Seatoller. It was the first day of his annual holiday and, eager to clear the soot of London out of his lungs and to feel hard rock under his boots, he had left word that he intended to walk to Wasdale by Sty Head, then by Black Sail Pass and Scarth Gap to Buttermere in time to catch the afternoon coach to Keswick.

Unhindered by cloud, a fierce sun beat down onto the thick tweed of his suit and, when he called at the popular hostelry of William Ritson at Wasdale Head, and was "by that well-known guide directed as to the proper route to pursue", Ritson noticed that he looked weary and advised him to rest; but, worried that he might miss the coach in Buttermere, he refused. In blistering heat, Edward Barnard set off up the valley and was never seen alive again.

When he failed to return to his hotel, a search party was organised; a local shepherd and several helpers were engaged to search the head of Ennerdale and over Haystacks and Scarth Gap, but they found nothing. Rumours started that he was not on the fells at all, but had 'run away'. Alarmed by the rumours and fearing that the local men might lose interest and stop searching,

James Barnard, the missing man's cousin, offered a reward of £50 to anyone who found the missing man, and placed an advertisement in the local newspapers:-

To the Shepherds of Cumberland

I who have been several days in this search, feel that we must look to you. Do not let it drop because you hear the missing man has taken himself off. I knew him and he was not a man to do so. Be assured he is somewhere on your fell, and as brave men with tender hearts for his poor waiting lady exert yourselves to clear up this sad mystery.

Letters flooded into the Times, each outlining a theory as to the whereabouts of the "missing tourist". Most favoured the belief that he had missed the Black Sail path and continued up Mosedale Beck to Wind Gap and descended into Ennerdale. This theory was strengthened when 'a sandwich and a half' was found, wrapped in newspaper, on Steeple. A big search was launched but nothing was found. Weeks passed and the enthusiasm of the searchers wore thin, but James Barnard was still convinced that his cousin lay somewhere on the fell.

In September, almost a full month after Edward Barnard disappeared, a shepherd stumbled on his body below Green Cove, not far from the river Liza. At a Coroner's inquest, held at Gatesgarth, the verdict was that he had died from heat-stroke.

A large cairn, about eight feet high, was erected on the spot where the body was found.

Birkett's Monument - Ullswater

Inscription

In Memory of
Norman William Birkett
Baron of Ulverston
He loved Ullswater
He strove to
Maintain its Beauty
For all to enjoy

O.S. Map: English Lakes NE 1:25000   **Grid ref:** 434204
Grade: C - by boat
Location
The plaque is attached to Kailpot Crag which rises out of Ullswater
on the south side of Howtown Bay. A popular footpath to the crag
contours round the foot of Hallin Fell from the Howtown-
Martindale road; but, though the panorama of the lake and hills
from the path is breathtaking, the plaque is tantalisingly hidden
from view and can only be reached by boat. There are a number of
boat hire operators around Ullswater.
Information
Norman Birkett, later Lord Birkett of Ulverston, was born at

14

Ulverston, then in Lancashire but now in Cumbria, in September 1883. His father was a draper who built up a chain of shops, and in 1898 Norman joined him in the family business but, seven years later, he left home with the intention of becoming a Wesleyan minister. While at Cambridge University, his eloquence at student debates led him away from a life as a minister of religion to a distinguished career as an eminent lawyer. He made history as the defence lawyer in spectacular criminal cases such as the trial of Dr Buck Ruxton and the infamous war criminals at Nuremburg, but to lovers of the Lake District he is best remembered for his vigorous campaign, with the support of Lord Lonsdale and the Ullswater Preservation Society, against Manchester Corporation's 1962 bid to impound Ullswater as a reservoir. The Government supported the Bill but, before a packed House of Lords, Norman Birkett made an impassioned speech, during which he said:-

" We have only to look at Thirlmere as it is today; we have only to look at Haweswater as it is today. Both lovely lakes have been murdered. They are now dead reservoirs: no human life; sterile shores; why, even the afforestation of the Manchester Corporation prevents proper access to the fell-side......And they come to this House with this Bill now and say, "we are only going to destroy a valley, if you can call it destruction; in Bannisdale, we are going to build a huge reservoir with a mighty dam; but it is a secluded valley, very few people go there" - as though seclusion and solitude was not one of things people wanted!......Under this Bill it can be taken for certainty - everybody with any experience of Lakeland knows it - that these lovely shores of Ullswater, where people picnic, where the ponies come down, will be just sterile shore like one sees at Thirlmere......The National Parks were set up so that the scenic beauty should be preserved and that the enjoyment of the parks should be for all people in all times.....So, far from saying in this House "It has been done many times. Let it be done once more," surely the argument should be "It has been done too many times already; do not let us add to it."
His stirring words won the day and Ullswater was saved; but, tragically, his triumph was short-lived. The following day he was taken ill, and three days later he died.

The Ullswater Preservation Society proposed that a plaque in his memory should be set into the rock face of Kailpot Crag, near Howtown on the eastern shore of Ullswater, and it was unveiled in the presence of two hundred guests from one of the lake steamers by Major E.W. Hassell, the Society's Chairman. The Society also proposed that a fell known as Nameless Fell, above the western shore, be renamed 'Birkett Fell'; and as the steamer slowly returned to Glenridding pier and the fell came into view, a party of boys from the Ullswater Outward Bound Mountain School, who had built a cairn and installed a plaque on the summit, fired Very lights into the sky.

Birkett Fell Plaque

Inscription

Birkett Fell

O.S. Map: English Lakes NE 1:25000   **Grid ref:** 364197
Grade: C
Location

The quickest way to reach Birkett Fell is by the path from Dowthwaitehead to Glenridding. Follow the path as it contours round the side of Birkett Fell to a kissing gate in a fence. Beyond the kissing gate resist the temptation to stay on the path and strike up the fell, making your own way to a wall on the summit, behind which is the prominent cairn.

The Bishop and the Clerk - Thornthwaite

The Bishop   The Clerk

Inscription   None

O.S. Map: English Lakes NW 1: 25000   **Grid ref:** 217265
Grade: C - but see Note
Location
On the south side of the prominent fell called Barf, opposite the Swan Hotel at Thornthwaite near Keswick.
Information
Although historians dispute all the numerous variations of the story of the pinnacle known as 'The Bishop's Rock', visible to passing motorists heading west from Keswick along the A66, the one most favoured in local folklore tells how the newly-appointed Bishop of Derry met his end while travelling to Whitehaven in 1783 to take passage to his diocese in Ireland. Breaking his journey at the Swan hotel, Thornthwaite, he apparently over-indulged in liquid hospitality and boasted to his fellow guests that he could ride his horse to the top of Barf and on to Lords Seat, two very steep hills immediately above the hotel. Bets were made and a crowd gathered to watch as the inebriated Bishop spurred his horse up the side of Barf, but when he reached the rock, now known as 'The Bishop's Rock', the horse stumbled and fell killing itself and the

rider. According to legend, the Bishop and his horse were buried together at the foot of the scree and the place marked with a rock named 'The Clerk'.

The Bishop's ill-fated ride is remembered by a clause written into the deeds of the hotel which requires the landlord of 'The Swan' to have the rocks whitewashed every year. Originally the payment to the person or persons who whitewashed the stones was 5 shillings and a quart of ale, but today this price is negotiable!

In 1984 the painting of the 'Bishop' was undertaken by two officers and four recruits of the King's Own Royal Border Regiment who were exercising in the area at the time the job became due, and since then the Army has largely taken over the task.

The 1987 whitewash was carried out by the Royal Engineer Corps from Cheshire, who volunteered to paint the Rock as one of the events to celebrate the 200th Anniversary of the granting of the title "Royal" to the Corps of Engineers. A thorough job was done with the 'Bishop' having both his back and front whitewashed.

Soldiers of the King's Own Royal Border Regiment usually whitewash the stones every September, though in 1997 Coniston Mountain Rescue Team took on the job as part of their 50th Anniversary Headquarters Extension Appeal. Some of the team members ascended the rock, 500 feet above the Swan Hotel, while others manned a display of ancient and modern rescue equipment outside the hotel.

In the 17th century the 'Swan Hotel' was called 'The Swan with two Necks' (the then licensee was Robert Cowen who combined his work as a publican with that of an 'animal preserver'.) A swan with two necks is the crest of the Worshipful Company of Vintners. The expression 'with two necks' really means 'two nicks', that is, two special marks on the beaks to denote the difference between the Vintners' Swans on the Thames and those of the King.

Note:
The 'Clerk' is easily reached but the approach to the 'Bishop' is very steep and exposed and is not recommended.

18

The Blencathra White Cross - Threlkeld

Inscription   None

O.S. Map: English Lakes NW 1:25000   **Grid ref:** 324281
Grade: A
Location
   On the 'Saddleback', a short distance north of Hallsfell (Blencathra) summit. The safest way to reach it is by the popular, but strenuous, path up Blease Fell from Threlkeld.
Information
   There are so many stone crosses on the summit of Blencathra it could easily be mistaken for a burial ground. There are numerous theories about their origin; and the large white stone (quartz) cross, about 5 metres long by 3 metres wide, is said to have been in memory of a fell-walker who was killed on the fell many years ago. It was originally much smaller in size. It is generally acknowledged that the cross was enlarged by the late Harold Robinson of Threlkeld, in memory of his friends who died in the 1939/45 war. For some mysterious reason the head of the large cross points to Lonscale

19

Fell on Skiddaw.

Close to the large white cross is a smaller slate one, with its head pointing towards the Pennine Range. On the southern slope of the Saddle, below the summit of Hallsfell Top, there is another, though smaller, white cross of unknown origin and, equally mysterious, there is a slate cross on the south side of Foule Crag close by the descent to Sharp Edge.

The monument builder Harold Robinson also left his mark in Blease Gill. Above Threlkeld car park the path crosses Blease Gill by a wooden bridge, then ascends a staircase built by the National Park Rangers. On a rock on the right, halfway up the staircase, Harold has carved his name and that of his brother Sid, together with a fox, a horse shoe, the Union Jack, and the date 1926.

Brandlehow Monument - Derwentwater

Inscription

The first property of the National Trust in this District
was opened on 16th October 1902 by H.R.H. The Princess
Louise. Four oaks were planted here by
Princess Louise
Miss Octavia Hill
Sir Robert Hunter
Canon H. D. Rawnsley

O.S. Map: English Lakes NW 1:25000   **Grid ref:** 248204
Grade: C
Location
The Portinscale to Grange road, skirting below Cat Bells, runs
alongside a wood on the left, then beside a large field before
Brandlehow Wood is reached. In the field, close to the road, will be
seen the four oak trees and a gate giving access to them. The
monument lies on the ground in the trees.

Information

Brandlehow Estate, with its very beautiful woodland and lakeside paths, was the first property in the Lake District to be acquired by the National Trust, and the £7,000 purchase price was raised following a public appeal by Miss Octavia Hill in 1900. Princess Louise, Duchess of Argyll and sister of King Edward V11, agreed to perform the opening ceremony and on the 6th of October 1902 the Cumberland Pacquet reported:-

'Her Royal Highness Princess Louise (Duchess of Argyll), who, with her husband, is staying with the Earl and Countess of Lonsdale at Lowther Castle, journeyed to Keswick on Thursday and as Vice president of the National Trust for the Preservation of Places of Historic Interest and Natural Beauty, performed an interesting ceremony. This was the dedication to public use and enjoyment of the Brandlehow Estate, an area of 108 acres of woodland and pasture, on the south-western shores of Lake Derwentwater.

The estate, which commands a mile or more of the south-western shore came unexpectedly into the market early in the spring of last year: and it is due largely, if not entirely, to the foresight of the Rev. Canon Rawnsley, vicar of Crosthwaite (the Parish Church of Keswick), that this natural park is now the people's possession; and to his zeal and personal effort - for he travelled many miles and addressed many meetings in the northern counties - may be ascribed the vigorous public opinion in favour of the scheme. Six months were given by the owner to raise £6,500 for the purchase (from an individual buyer he would have demanded £7,000): but five months had not elapsed before £7,516 came to hand - sufficient to complete the purchase, with the accompanying law expense of transfer, and to form the nucleus of a maintenance fund.

The Rev. Canon Rawnsley presented an address of welcome engrossed on white vellum and enclosed in a silver casket. This mentioned that the number of subscribers to the purchase fund exceeded 1,300, and "not the least pleasing incident of the raising of the money was that a great many of the working men and women of our northern towns sent small subscriptions, and it was evident a real feeling exists that the preservation of this beautiful scenery is of national moment."

Her Royal Highness and the Duke of Argyll afterwards planted memorial trees, and others were planted by Sir Robert Hunter, Miss Octavia Hill and Canon Rawnsley. The band of the 1st V. B. Border Regiment was in attendance, and played the National Anthem as the party entered and left the grounds.'

Notes on the founders of the National Trust

Canon Rawnsley - see page 89

Octavia Hill - born in 1838, one of five daughters of a corn merchant in Wisbech, Cambridgeshire. Owing to her father's illness after losing his business, the family moved to London where Octavia qualified as a teacher and taught in a school for young ladies run by her mother. She became closely involved with the plight of poor people and, having tried unsuccessfully to open a lodging house where families with small children could shelter, she turned to the wealthy John Ruskin for help. He bought several properties for her in the London slums and had them renovated. She ran her scheme according to strict rules and from it, in 1869, was formed the Charity Organization Society, later the Family Welfare Trust. Her concern that people living in urban places should have room for recreation and exercise led to her proposing, at a meeting in London in July, 1894 attended by many wealthy and influential people, 'that it is desirable to provide means by which landowners and others may be enabled to dedicate to the nation places of historic interest or natural beauty.' Her proposal fired the enthusiasm of 'the most active volcano in Europe', the Rev. Canon Rawnsley, and Sir Robert Hunter, a London lawyer and an authority on commons and public rights. Together, in 1895, they founded the National Trust for the Preservation of Places of Historic Interest and Natural Beauty.

In 1902, in a letter to her mother, she wrote 'A song of thankfulness seems to be singing in my heart for having been given power to have some hand in devoting some of the lovely places to the people for ever.' Octavia Hill died in 1912 at the age of 74, and a hundred acres of heath and woodland at Godalming in Surrey was dedicated to her memory by the National Trust.

Sir Robert Hunter - born in London in 1844, and, after taking an M.A. degree in 1865, studied law and became a partner in a firm of solicitors who represented the Commons Preservation Society. He won many cases which led to the protection of threatened commons and open spaces, and established the principles on which the law relating to commons is now based. In 1882 he was appointed solicitor to the General Post Office, but maintained his interest in protecting commons and was closely associated with the Commons Preservation Society. He was knighted in 1894, and when he died at Haslemere in 1913, at the age of 69, a nearby woodland was purchased by public subscription as a memorial to his work.

The 'Brandy' and 'Patch' Memorials
Buttermere

Inscription

In Memory of
BRANDY
from his climbing friends

O.S. Map: English Lakes NW 1:25000   **Grid ref:** 193162
Grade: C - but see warning
Location
   Hassness, on the north shore of Buttermere, is renowned for its
hospitable guest house, its intriguing rock tunnel, and a superb,
picturesque rocky gorge, down which thunders Hassnesshow beck.
From a kissing gate with a sign 'public footpath', opposite Hassness
House, a well-trodden path keeps close to the beck and climbs
through a wood to a stile. Over the stile the path continues up the
open fell with views of the gorge that make photographers leap for
their cameras. Watch carefully for a thin path which branches left
off the main path, crosses a beck and heads for a small concrete
dam - the water supply for Hassness. On the right hand side of the
dam, scramble a short distance up rock and heather and the plaque
to 'Brandy' will be seen fastened to a small, rocky outcrop. The

plaque to 'Patch' is a short distance above it, half hidden on a ledge at the edge of the gorge. WARNING - the plaque to 'Brandy' is safe and easy to reach, but the plaque to 'Patch' is in an exposed position above the ghyll and to reach it requires great care. It is no place for children or dogs.

Information

Joseph Jared of Aughton, Ormskirk, Lancashire, replying to an enquiry about Brandy in the magazine 'Cumbria', wrote:-
'Brandy' was the much-loved Golden Cocker Spaniel of the owners of a local hotel. A 'Cragsman Extraordinary' he accompanied guests of his choice on their ramblings and scramblings in the area. He made many friends. Run over by a car, he survived but could no longer roam his beloved fells. He died and it was thought that he had eaten poisonous vegetation. His many friends wondered if he had 'ended it all'. He was buried in the hotel grounds under a local slate headstone inscribed 'Brandy, everyone's friend'. Some of his friends whom he had 'preferred' placed the plaque in a gully in the valley he loved so much.

'Patch' was a cross Alsatian/Border Collie who was born in 1971 and who was the faithful friend of Derek Tunstall, a National Park Voluntary Warden and a member of Cockermouth Mountain Rescue Team. Patch was never happier than when he was snuffling around the crags, and was greatly missed when he died. He is remembered by a plaque in a place where only brave dogs dare tread.

The Brothers Stone - Helvellyn

Inscription

Here did we stop and here looked round
While each into himself descends
For that last thought of parting friends
That is not to be found.
Brother and friend, if verse of mine
Have power to make thy virtues known
Here let a monumental stone
Stand - sacred as a shrine

O.S. Map: English Lakes NE 1:25000   **Grid ref:** 353124
Grade: B

Location

Carved on the side of a large rock a short distance north east of Grisedale Tarn, close by the right hand side of the path down Grisedale to Patterdale. Above the rock there is a metal plaque fastened to a metal post and inscribed 'The Brothers Parting'.

Information

The poet William Wordsworth was very close to his brother John, who was a sea captain. In 1800, John spent an enjoyable eight months at Grasmere with his brother, his sister Dorothy and his future sister-in-law Mary. During his stay he became rather fond of Mary's sister Sara Hutchinson, and it was always his wish that he would earn enough money to be able to support William in his writing and perhaps retire to Grasmere and marry Sara. In September 1800 before John left to join his ship, the two brothers walked along the old pack-horse track from Grasmere to Patterdale; and near Grisedale Tarn they sat silently against a rock, each dwelling unhappily on John's imminent departure. Lamentably, John's voyage was a financial disaster; but when William saw him briefly in London he was optimistic that his next voyage would be a success and, as William wrote later, 'he went to sea again, with the same hope of being useful to us.' Alas, this voyage was also a failure.

But Captain John Wordsworth's nickname amongst his officers was 'the Philosopher' and, characteristically, in a letter to William from Portsmouth in January 1805, he was full of hope and wrote that he was about to set sail as master of the East India Company's ship, the Earl of Abergavenny. John had often told William that he distrusted Pilots, and on the 6th of February, while on passage down the English Channel with a Pilot on board, the Earl of Abergavenny was driven onto the rocks off Portland Bill on the Devon coast, and John and several of his crew were drowned. William was utterly devastated and wrote to his friend Sir George Beaumont:-

'I write to you from a house of mourning. My poor sister, and wife, who loved him almost as we did, are in miserable affliction, which I do all in my power to alleviate; but heaven knows I want consolation myself. I can say nothing higher of my ever dear brother than that he was......meek, affectionate, silently enthusiastic, loving all quiet things, and a poet in every thing but words.'

Deeply shaken by the death of his brother at the age of 32, William expressed his grief in the way he knew best and wrote a number of poems including the Elegiac Verses, in which he finds comfort in John's favourite mountain flowers that grew around Grisedale Tarn.

In 1888 Canon Rawnsley persuaded the Wordsworth Society to commemorate the sad parting of the brothers on that Michaelmas Day of 1800, and in true Rawnsley fashion he afterwards wrote:-

'One hundred yards from Grisedale Tarn on a large mass of rock I was able, on behalf of the Wordsworth Society, to have roughly engraved two verses from Wordsworth's Elegiac Verses.'

Cecil Spring Rice Bridge - Ullswater

Inscription

In Affectionate Remembrance of Cecil Spring Rice, GCMG - GCVO Poet, Privy Councillor, H. M. Ambassador to the United States of America during the Great War. This Bridge has been set up by Members of his Family, by his Friends, and by his Colleagues of the Diplomatic Service AD 1931. Born in London 1859, lived at Old Church Ullswater. Died in Ottowa Canada 1919

'No Ambassador has ever had to discharge duties of greater delicacy or of more far reaching importance than fell to his lot. Nor has any Ambassador ever fulfilled his task with more unwearied vigilance, conspicuous ability and ultimate success'
Speech by Lord Robert Cecil, House of Commons 1918

O.S. Map: English Lakes NW 1:25000   **Grid ref:** 400210
Grade: C
Location
Follow the footpath from the National Trust's car park at Aira Force, Ullswater, on the Glenridding - Pooley Bridge road.

Information

High up in the magnificent gorge of Aira Force, there are two superb local stone bridges which were built as memorials to members of the Spring Rice family, who lived at Old Church, a small estate near Watermillock, Ullswater - now the Old Church Hotel. The lower of the two bridges is in memory of Sir Cecil Arthur Spring Rice, who was born in London in 1859 and was the grandson of Thomas, the first Baron Monteagle of Brandon, in Kerry, a politician who represented Limerick from 1820-1839. It was he who introduced the penny postage scheme into Britain in 1839. The Spring Rice family connection with Ullswater was established through his second marriage to the eldest daughter of John Marshall of Hallsteads, Patterdale. His son Charles, by his first wife, strengthened the Ullswater connection by marrying Elizabeth, the daughter of William Marshall M.P. of Hallsteads, Patterdale, and at their Ullswater estate they enjoyed visits from Ruskin, Sir Walter Scott and the Wordsworths.

Charles and Elizabeth had eight children and their second son, Cecil, entered the Foreign Office in 1882, serving in Berlin, Cairo, St Petersburg, Persia and Washington, and was knighted in 1906. While in Russia he married Florence, the only daughter of Sir Frank Lascelles, and they had a son and a daughter. He acted as a conciliatory influence between Gt Britain and the United States during the 1914-18 war and it is believed that it was his tact and diplomacy during delicate negotiations that brought America into the war on the side of the UK. He was a personal friend of Theodore Roosevelt and his family and was Best Man at his wedding. Cecil was known as 'Springy' to his friends, and Roosevelt's sister, Lady Helen Ferguson, jokingly christened his children the 'offspringies'. In January 1918 he left Washington for Canada to rest; but the strain of three and a half years ceaseless work and anxiety had undermined his health and, the following month, while waiting at Ottowa for a ship to take him home, he died suddenly and was buried in Canada.

A gifted poet, he had several books of his poems published. He had a great affection for the Lake District and loved tramping the fells around Ullswater. He was inspired by the beauty of this lake to describe it in a poem, but it was in Canada on the 12th of

January 1918, only a few days before he died, that he wrote two verses for which he will always be remembered. His poem 'I vow to thee my country' was later put to the music of 'Jupiter' from Gustav Holst's Planets Suite, and was, and is still, popular as a patriotic song.

I vow to thee, my country - all earthly things above
Entire and whole and perfect, the service of my love,
The love that asks no questions: the love that stands the test,
That lays upon the altar the dearest and the best:
The love that never falters, the love that pays the price,
The love that makes undaunted the final sacrifice.

And there's another country, I've heard of long ago-
Most dear to them that love her, most great to them that know-
We may not count her armies: we may not see her King-
Her fortress is a faithful heart, her pride is suffering-
And soul by soul and silently her shining bounds increase,
And her ways are ways of gentleness and all her paths are
    peace

The upper one of the two Aira Force bridges was built in memory of Stephen Spring Rice, Cecil's elder brother who died in 1902, and of Gerald, a younger brother, killed in the 1914-18 war. Due to his age, almost 50, Gerald had been turned down for war service in 1914, but through family contacts he managed to get into the army as a lieutenant in the transport service of the Border Regiment. He was wounded and invalided home but, as soon as he was fit, he returned to his regiment and, in May 1916, was killed by a shell in France.

Stephen and Gerald's Bridge

31

Chandravadan Parekh's Monument
Stonethwaite

Inscription

We have set up this stone in memory of our dear friend Chandravadan Parekh aged 15 years who came down with us from High Raise and died of exposure near this place on March 18th 1968. Our attempts to help him were unsuccessful and by his shattering death he has made us forever humbler and more gentle in our lives.

David Atkinson   Hillary Hutchinson
David Baron   Peter John Ingrams
Graham Birkett   Stuart Maugh
Charles Dixon   David Murray

May 1968

And Death shall have no Dominion

O.S. Map: English Lakes NW 1:25000   **Grid ref:** 279125
Grade: B
Location
   Approx. 1.25 miles up Greenup Gill from Stonethwaite, Borrowdale. Go past Hallworth's Bridge at Smithymire Island and continue along the track to a gate in a wall. Beyond the gate the path crosses a beck and starts to climb a boulder-covered slope. Walk up the boulder slope, keeping the path on your right and the beck on your left, and keep looking left for a large boulder, set in the hillside, half covered in grass and moss. The plaque is concealed on the north side of it.
Information
   On March the 18th 1968, a party of teenage boys from a private school near Carlisle set out with their headmaster for a day walking the fells on the east side of Borrowdale. It was a typical raw March day, cold, with showers of hail and a nasty wind, but the walk from the summit of Ullscarf, 2370', by way of Greenup Edge and Low White Stones, 2341', to High Raise, 2500', was well within the capabilities of a group adequately equipped for the time of year. The party had climbed Ullscarf and Low White Stones but, when only about 100 yards from the the top of High Raise, the head-master noticed that 15 year old Chandravadan Parekh, an Asian lad from Birmingham, was very tired and having difficulty walking. He decided to cut short the walk and head down into Greenup Gill, but the party had only gone a few hundred yards when Parekh sat down and said he could not go on. The headmaster gave him a teaspoonful of brandy and carried him down the fell for a short distance; but it was too much for one person and, telling the rest of the boys to put Parekh in a sleeping bag and carry him down the best they could, the Headmaster ran down the valley to bring their vehicle as close to the bottom of the fell as he could.
   Unfortunately, by the time the party managed to reach Stonethwaite Parekh appeared to be lifeless, and though the Superintendent of the Keswick branch of the St John Ambulance Brigade applied artificial respiration, it was unsuccessful. The inquest found that he had died from exposure.

Chapels Monument - Ravenglass

Inscription   None
O.S. Map: English Lakes SW 1:25000   **Grid ref:** 111975
Grade: C
Location
   The owners of Muncaster Castle regret that they are unable to permit public access to the monument as it is in a poor state of repair. However, a good view of it can be had from the public bridleway which starts at Muncaster Chase, a short distance south of Muncaster Castle main gate. The path climbs towards Muncaster Fell, but when it levels out by Muncaster Tarn it turns at right angles and after a few metres joins a wall descending past Chapels Cottages and the monument. On your way back, Muncaster Castle and the Owl Centre are worth a visit.
Information
   1464 was a memorable year for the Penningtons of Muncaster Castle. Two shepherds were going about their work at a place called Chapels, a short distance east of the castle, when they came upon a

man, mud-stained and weary, who asked to be directed to Muncaster Castle. The shepherds took him to the castle where the then Lord of the Manor, Sir John Pennington, discovered the traveller to be no less a person than King Henry V1, who, having been defeated in battle at Hexham in Northumberland, was making his escape. He had been refused shelter at Irton Hall near Holmrook, and set off over the fell to Muncaster. Sir John readily gave the unfortunate monarch shelter, and he stayed at the castle for a short time before setting off on his ill-fated journey through Lancashire, where he was betrayed by a monk and captured.

On leaving Muncaster Castle, the King gave Sir John a small glass bowl, saying that the Penningtons would enjoy good fortune as long as the bowl remained intact. Looking after a glass bowl, at a time when successive invaders were sweeping up and down Cumberland knocking down castles, was no easy task; but somehow the Penningtons managed it, and the 'Luck of Muncaster' as the bowl is known, still survives.

A superb tower was built on the spot where the King was found, and it is to be hoped that English Heritage will recognise its value as an ancient monument and rescue it before it is too late.

Dick Marsh Bridge - Eskdale

Inscription

This bridge was built
in memory of
Dick Marsh
Aged 38
who in August 1964
lost his life climbing
in these mountains.

O.S. Map: English lakes SW 1:25000   **Grid ref:** 213014
Grade: C
Location
    The bridge spans the river Esk between Brotherilkeld farm and Taw House farm at the foot of Hardknott Pass, Eskdale.
Information
    A keen mountaineer, Richard Marsh developed a taste for Himalayan climbing when he was in the army in India. In 1950, at the age of twenty four, he set off with two friends, Jim Thornley and Bill Crace, to spend a year exploring, surveying and climbing in an un-mapped region of the Karakoram Mountains on the northern borders of Pakistan. The Pakistan Government sanctioned the expedition; but, after a gruelling trek, the party reached the edge of the region only to be told that permission had been cancelled and they were ordered to return. Having invested £2000 in the expedition,

the trio were determined not to return home with nothing achieved, and decided to tackle the then unclimbed peak of Nanga Parbat, 26,660 feet high and with a notorious reputation for bad weather and avalanches, which had already caused a number of mountaineering disasters. High on the mountain, Dick Marsh's feet suffered badly from frostbite and he was forced to go down to a lower altitude. His two companions decided to carry on for the summit, and were never seen again.

Returning to the UK, Dick Marsh worked for a number of years as the Chief Instructor of the Outward Bound Mountain School in Eskdale. He left to become ordained, and eventually took the post of Warden of a Church of England Centre at Scargill, in the Yorkshire Dales. One of the courses run by the Centre was for fathers and sons, and Dick Marsh believed that by taking them rock-climbing they would develop understanding and respect for each other.

It was while pursuing his love of rock-climbing that Dick Marsh met his death as mysteriously as his two friends on Nanga Parbat. On September 4th, 1964, the Westmorland Gazette reported:-

'Two climbers were killed in a fall from 350 foot Dow Crag, Coniston, on Friday. They were the Rev. Richard Michael Waring Marsh, age 38, of Scargill House, Kettlewell, Skipton, a married man with two children and Leslie Ashburn, aged 30, of Saxby Street, Salford, a theological student. The bodies of the two men, roped together, were found at the foot of "C" Buttress by a Dumfries doctor and his family.'

No one can be certain what happened; but, at the inquest, witnesses said that the rock was greasy and it was possible that one of the men had fallen and pulled his companion with him.

John Lagoe, who worked at the Outward Bound School, Eskdale at the same time as Dick Marsh, together with Ian, later Bishop, Griggs, an Eskdale instructor and Roger Sawtell, a close friend, wanted to set up a memorial to Dick Marsh and in 1970, with financial help from the Marsh family and through the combined efforts of Cumberland County Council, the National Trust and the Lake District Planning Board, a bridge was built across the River Esk at Brotherilkeld. The beams were of Corten steel and lasted well, but the wood rotted with time and was completely replaced by National Trust craftsmen in 1997. Cumbria County Council and the Lakes National Park Authority shared the cost.

Dixon's Monument - Helvellyn

Inscription

In Memory of
Robert Dixon
Rookings, Patterdale
Who was killed on this
place on the 27th Day
of November 1858 when
following the Patterdale
Foxhounds

O.S. Map: English Lakes NE 1:25000   **Grid ref:** 349149

Grade: A

Location

On Striding Edge ridge. A metal plaque attached to a metal post on a ledge. Easy to pass without seeing it. Best way to approach is along the well-used path from Patterdale; but should only be attempted by experienced walkers in good weather.

Information

On December the 7th 1858 the Cumberland Pacquet reported:-
'A few days since, a very serious accident occurred near Patterdale, which has cast a gloom over the inhabitants of that village. The unfortunate individual was Robert Dixon, youngest son of the late Mr. John Dixon, Yeoman, of Crookabeck, in Patterdale, who, with others, went out in the morning to have a day's sport with Mr J Mounsey's fox-hounds. When going along the narrow ridge called Striding Edge, which leads up to and joins Helvellyn, and at the highest and steepest place, known by the name of High Spying Howe, Dixon's foot slipped, and he was precipitated down the steep precipice towards Nethermost Cove, among the rocks and shingle. There were two or three companions with him at the time, who hastened to the place where he had fallen, and found him with his head lying downwards, and to all appearances dead. It was found, however, that he breathed. They took him up and bore him down towards Elmhow, which was a difficult task, owing to the way being so rugged. A cart was then secured, into which they put a bed, and then placed him upon it, and conveyed him home. He was quite unconscious, and never spoke after he fell. Dr Rumney attended, but found him past recovery. He was 33 years of age, a strong, healthy young man, and a keen sportsman.'

His brother, Birkett, had a monument cast in iron and fixed to the spot where he fell.

Donald Campbell Monument - Ullswater

Inscription
Marking the place where DONALD CAMPBELL CBE launched his boat BLUEBIRD and achieved the water speed record of 202.32 mph on July 23 1955.
"Into the water barrier and beyond"
Placed by the Glenridding Hotel and Ullswater Navigation and unveiled by GINA CAMPBELL on 21 October 1997

O.S. Map: English Lakes NE 1:25000   **Grid ref:** 390169
Grade: C
Location
Ullswater Navigation slipway, Glenridding, Ullswater.
Information
The attempts on the world water speed record by Donald Campbell and his boat Bluebird have such strong associations with Coniston Water that his achievements on Ullswater are often over-looked.

Having reached a speed of 141 mph on Coniston in 1950, just half a mile an hour slower than the record set by his father, Sir Malcolm Campbell, eleven years previously, 29 year old Donald returned to Coniston the following year to try again. By then he had already spent £10,000 trying to achieve his ambition: but once again glory was snatched from him when, after unofficially breaking the world record with a speed of 165 mph, his boat hit an obstacle and sank.

Four years and a further £25,000 later, a new Bluebird - designed by Kenneth and Lewis Norris of Burgess Hill, Sussex and built around a Metro-Vickers jet engine by Salmesbury Engineering Company, near Blackburn - was ready for testing; and in January 1955 it was transported by road to Ullswater, where Campbell had set up a base at the Glenridding Hotel. Campbell's team set to work testing and modifying the boat and he took it out for a slow run in February. A month later he made a run of over 100 mph and further testing continued until, at the beginning of July, he decided the boat was ready for a record bid. His father's record of 141 mph had been topped by an American, Stanley S. Sayers, with 179.497 mph; but Campbell was confident that in his new Bluebird he had a world beater.

Saturday the 23rd of July was the date set for the bid; but to Campbell's dismay a stiff breeze blew all morning, and to while away the time he played chess in the hotel. Miraculously the wind dropped towards midday and, steering Bluebird out onto the lake for the first of the two compulsory runs, Campbell gave the engine full throttle and screeched the length of the measured kilometre in a cloud of spray at an incredible speed of 215.08 mph. His second run, half an hour later, was slower at 189.57 mph, but the average for the two was a fantastic 202.32 mph. He had achieved a new world water speed record, and when it was officially announced the crowds of spectators around the lake went wild with excitement.

Up to that time only two other men, Britain's John Cobb and Italy's Mario Verga, had travelled at over 200 mph on water, and both were killed when their boats disintegrated.

The water speed record had come a long way since the first official record was set up, in 1903 , by S.F. Edge at a cracking speed of 19.53 mph !

There is a library and a small exhibition of memorabilia dedicated to Campbell on display in the Glenridding Hotel.

Dorothy Well - Portinscale

Inscription

On the small well :-
> Whosoever drinketh of this water shall thirst again
> But whosoever drinketh of the water that
> I shall give him shall never thirst

O.S. Map: English Lakes NW 1:25000   **Grid ref:** 252236
Grade: C
Location
   Portinscale village, in front of Dalegarth House Hotel
Information
   Many hundreds of visiting motorists whiz through the old- world village of Portinscale unaware they have passed within feet of two beautifully restored wells, set side by side. In days gone by, the wells were the village's only water supply and were provided by the Rev. Thomas Christian, who was the Vicar of Crosthwaite Church, Keswick, from 1728 to 1758. He was the uncle of the

infamous Fletcher Christian, who led the mutiny on the British ship 'Bounty' in 1789. But long before the deeds of Fletcher Christian cast a cloud over the family, the Rev. Thomas suffered his own personal tragedy when his only daughter, Dorothy, who was unmarried and lived with her parents, died at the age of 42 in September 1772. In her memory he had the stone arches built over the wells, and on the smaller of the two he had the inscription carved into the stone.

For many years the wells were dilapidated and overgrown with weeds, but, in 1976, the local Parish Council commissioned Mr Jim Little, of Keswick, to restore what is now a very attractive village landmark.

Dr John's Seat - Rosthwaite

Inscription

In Memory of
"Dr. John"
(Medical Officer)
(Keswick M.R.T.)
From His Many
Climbing And
Other Friends

O.S. Map: English Lakes NW 1:25000   **Grid ref:** 259149
Grade: C
Location
Next to the bus stop by Rosthwaite post office, Borrowdale.
Information
    A list of memorial seats to be found in the Lake District would
fill several volumes and we decided not to include any in this book.
But, occasionally, they are memorials to very exceptional and
dedicated people. Dr John Lyth was one of them. A tribute to him

in an annual report of the Keswick Mountain Rescue Team says:-
'The Team has been exceptionally fortunate in its medical officers. The pattern of active participation and constant training was set by Dr. Lyth, founder member of the Team and its medical officer until 1963.'

Dr. John, as he was widely known, joined many a rescue and, even when he was no longer able to go on the fell, he would wait at an advanced base in case his skills were required when a casualty was brought down. His loyalty lasted until the end. Only hours before he died, he went to Lairthwaite School to give a first-aid demonstration to four young members of the Team.

He was in general practice in York from 1912 to 1946, but his talents were not confined to medicine and mountains. Widely read and a keen student of the classics, he had considerable literary ability, best in evidence in his book of poems 'One More Cairn' published in 1954 . Anyone at home on the crags will surely echo the sentiments of:

> I have loved rock and all the things that go
> with climbing; I have loved the feel of rope
> To handle it alone, without the hope
> Of present use; the smooth, soft, even flow
> Of well-used nylon; or the rougher touch
> Betrayed by hemp, so it be stout and strong.

Dr. John's services to the community, and mountain rescue in particular, were acknowledged by a memorial seat at Rosthwaite, just at the start of the popular footpath to Watendlath.

Fanny Mercer's Cross - Buttermere

Inscription:

Erected by friends of Fanny Mercer accidentally killed
1887

O.S. Map: English Lakes NW 1:25000   **Grid ref:** 196147
Grade: C
Location:
   The B5289 road from Buttermere to Borrowdale passes Gatesgarth
Farm at the east end of the lake and emerges into a bleak, treeless
landscape bounded on both sides by steep crags. The long ridge
climbing skywards immediately on the right is Fleetwith Pike and,
near the base of the ridge, bolted to a ledge, is a white wooden
cross in memory of Fanny Mercer, who fell to her death while
descending the ridge in 1887. The cross is easily reached along a
prominent path which climbs Fleetwith Pike, but take care if you
have small children with you.

Information

The West Cumberland Times of 17 September 1887 reported :-
'On Thursday afternoon, 18 year old Fanny Mercer, one of the servants of Mr Bowden-Smith, one of the masters of Rugby School, who is at present residing at Wood House, Buttermere, was spending the afternoon on the hills in the company of Walter Clarke, butler with Mr Bowden-Smith, and Clara Tamer, a fellow servant. They went round by the east side of Warmes Crag to the top, right above Honister Quarries. They were coming down the ridge between the carriage road and the east side of the hill, and had got comparatively near the bottom. Miss Mercer was the highest on the ridge and Miss Tamer lowest, and Walter Clarke was in between them. Miss Mercer was going to get down to where Miss Tamer was standing and took hold of her alpenstock close to the top. She leaped off the ledge on which she was standing, but instead of sliding her hands down the alpenstock she clung to the top, with the natural consequence that she was carried on a considerable distance further than she had anticipated. She jumped right over Walter Clarke's head, and fell backwards, rolling 130 feet down the steep mountain side. Walter Clarke tried to grab hold of her dress but a portion of the garment was torn off and left in his hand. James Kennedy, a farm servant with Mrs Nelson, Gatesgarth was raking brackens on the opposite side of the hill and saw the party coming down the ridge. On witnessing the accident he ran across the hill and assisted to carry the body down. She was taken to Gatesgarth without delay and died before nine o clock.'

Fell & Rock Memorial Bridge - Ennerdale

Inscription

This bridge was reconstructed in 1959 by the Cumberland County Council. The Fell and Rock Climbing Club of the English Lake District bore a share of the cost in memory of those of its members who fell in the World War of 1939-1945.

O.S. Map: English Lakes NW 1:25000   **Grid ref:** 178131

Grade: C

Location

Spans the River Liza, below Pillar Rock, in the upper Ennerdale valley. A touch under five miles from the Forestry Commission's car park at Bowness Knott. Can be reached over Scarth Gap Pass from Buttermere or over Black Sail Pass from Wasdale, in which case the difficulty Grade for both is B.

Information

After the purchase of Great Gable and other fells by the Fell & Rock Climbing Club in 1924, £55 of the £600 subscribed remained in balance. By 1957, through the accumulation of interest, it had grown to £115 and Dick Plint, the then treasurer, wondered what it could be used for. When one of the club members mentioned that the Friends of the Lake District were considering launching an appeal to climbing and rambling clubs for funds to repair the bridge over the Liza on the track from Pillar Rock to Scarth Gap, it seemed the ideal opportunity for the surplus funds to be put to good use. The old bridge was in a poor condition, but no-one would accept responsibility for repairing it. The track was a right of way and therefore the responsibility of Cumberland County Council, but the proposal put forward by the Lake District Planning Board for repairing it had been rejected by the Highways Committee, who argued that the Forestry Commission had built it for their own use and that there was an adequate bridge 1 mile downstream, (the Forestry Commission's concrete road bridge.) By way of a compromise, the County Council offered to pay two thirds of the cost of a new bridge if Ennerdale Parish would pay one third, but the Parish Council couldn't raise the money. The Friends of the Lake District were about to launch their appeal to the clubs when the Fell & Rock Climbing Club saved the day with an offer to put up some of the cash needed to have a new bridge built, in memory of members who fell in the 1939-45 war.

Work on the new bridge went ahead and the formal opening was held on the 8th of May 1960, the anniversary of V E Day. Invitations to the opening ceremony were sent to those relatives who could be traced of the 13 club members who had fallen, together with officials of Cumberland County Council, the Forestry Commission and the Lake District Planning Board. The Forestry Commission relaxed its 'no unauthorised vehicles' rule to enable guests to be brought up to the bridge by car, and over 100 people walked over the fells from all directions to witness the opening of the new bridge and the unveiling of a bronze tablet fastened to a granite boulder. Preparation of the granite boulder before attaching the plaque is reputed to have taken the edge off twenty four chisels.

Mr John C. Appleyard, of Torver, was given the honour of unveiling the plaque, and the dedication was by another long-standing club member, the Rev. G. W. Ellison, Vicar of Langdale.

The cost of building the bridge was £582, the Club contributing nearly £200.

Fell & Rock Memorial Plaque - Great Gable

Inscription

In glorious and happy memory of those whose names are inscribed below, members of this club, who died for their country in the European War, 1914-18, these fells were acquired by their fellow-members and by them invested in the National Trust for the use and enjoyment of the people of our land for all time

J.S.Bainbridge: J.G.Bean: H.S.P.Blair: A.J.Clay: J.N.Fletcher: W.H. B.Gross: E Hartley: S.W.Herford: S.F.Jeffcoat: E.B.Lees: S.J. Linzell: L.J.Oppenheimer: A.J.Prichard: A.M.Rimer: R.B.Sanderson: H.L.Slingsby: G.C.Turner: B.H.Witty: J.H.Whitworth: C.S.Worthington

O.S. Map: English Lakes SW 1:25000   **Grid ref:** 211103
Grade: A
Location   Great Gable Summit Cairn

Information

At the end of the 1914-18 war, during which many members of the Fell and Rock Climbing Club of the English Lake District lost their lives, the club committee wanted to honour their memory with a memorial 'To last as long as the everlasting hills,' and in 1919 Herbert P. Cain, the Club's librarian, launched an appeal at Coniston with the slogan 'Let's Buy a Fell'. The first choice was Pillar, but the owner, Lord Lonsdale, refused to sell. In 1920, the Musgrave Estate, which included Napes Needle, the perfect monument to the memory of Lakeland climbers, came on the market, but the sale fell through.

About that time, Row Head Farm at Wasdale Head, which included Great Gable, was bought by Mr Herbert Walker of Seascale. Aware that he had once been a keen climber himself, and might be sympathetic, the Club Secretary sent him a map of his newly acquired property, with Great Gable and adjacent fells ringed in black, and an optimistic request that the Club be allowed to buy "all this over 1,500 feet, please."

Whether it was due to the sheer cheek of the request or Mr Walker's eagerness to support the cause is not recorded, but he offered all the land asked for at a price of £400, subject to certain conditions and reservations, mainly concerned with safeguarding the grazing rights of the farm tenant. Hardly daring to believe their luck, the Committee accepted and the following letter was sent to all club members:-

'The time has now come when it is the privilege of the Committee to put before you the War Memorial Scheme. After much delay, which they think you will consider to have been not without its compensation, they have negotiated for the purchase of a very large portion of the centre of climbing and walking in the district. This comprises the tops of twelve mountains, viz.:- Kirkfell, Great Gable, Green Gable, Brandreth, Grey Knotts, Base Brown, Seathwaite Fell, Glaramara, Allen Crags, Great End, Broad Crag and Lingmell, together with almost all the land over 1,500 feet, bounding them on the sides facing the Seathwaite to Wasdale track. The Committee have been most cordially met in their dealings with the owner, Herbert W. Walker, Esq., of Seascale.

Arrangements are being made to hand this whole area over to the National Trust, who will comply with the conditions laid down by the Club, and safeguard its interest in perpetuity. It has been considered desirable definitely to associate with this most appropriate memorial the names of those members who gave their lives in the War, and for this purpose a bronze tablet will be placed on, or near, the summit of Great Gable.The Committee confidently invite all members to support this memorial as generously as they can, realizing that in so doing they do honour to their comrades, while preserving to their successors for all time the finest area of fell and rock in England.'

400, out of a total membership of some 450, donated nearly £600. and in 1924 the purchase was completed. 'In glorious and happy memory of our fallen, the fairest portion of our own country had for all time been made safe for the use and enjoyment of its people'.

Folly Bridge - Seatoller

Inscription

The bridge was built at the
expence of John Braithwaite
of Seatoller in the year of
our Lord
1781
By Thomas Hayton and
Richard Bowness

I count this Folly you have done,
As you have neither Wife nor Son
Daughter I have, God give her grace
And Heaven for her resting place

O.S. Map: English Lakes NW 1:25000   **Grid ref:** 251139
Grade: C

Location

Behind Mountain View Cottages, Seatoller, Borrowdale

Information

In the 18th century there were several families of Braithwaites living in Borrowdale but, from our researches, we believe that the John Braithwaite who built Folly Bridge was the son of Joseph and Mary Braithwaite (nee Wren), who lived in Seatoller between 1760 and 1780. Joseph appears to have owned a lot of property in the area and could possibly have had shares in the Seathwaite wad mine. The will of Mary Braithwaite, widow, of Seatoller in Borrowdale, dated April 1779, states:-

'I give to my son John Braithwaite all my freehold estate house and land at Seatoller or elsewhere within the liberties of Borrowdale to hold for him the said John Braithwaite for his heirs and assigns for ever. I give and bequeath to Mary elder daughter of my son John Braithwaite the sum of £20 to be paid to her when she shall arrive at the age of 18 years together with my best featherbed, and furniture thereto belonging with my best brass kettle and also my best wainscot press - I give and bequeath to Sarah younger daughter of my son John Braithwaite the sum of £20 to be paid to her when she shall arrive at the age of 18 years and one other brass kettle and wainscot press.

She leaves six pence each to all the poor people who attend her funeral.'

The son John mentioned in the will married Elizabeth Ormandy from Grasmere in November 1776, and a year later a daughter, Mary, was born. In March 1779 another daughter, Sarah, was born; but the rejoicing was short-lived. In August, John's mother died, in September his daughter Mary died and was buried three days after her second birthday, and five months later, in February 1780, his wife Elizabeth died.

According to a story handed down in some Borrowdale families, little Mary was drowned in the pool under Folly Bridge. Could it be that her mother never recovered from the shock of the loss and died not long after?

Within the space of a few months John Braithwaite's mother, his daughter and his wife had been taken from him, and the only family he had left was Sarah, barely one year old. Perhaps the bridge was a memorial to his family and the curious inscription on the tablet, in which he appears to be addressing himself, reflects the state of his tortured mind.

Sarah Braithwaite lived on to marry Edward Fletcher of Salford, near Manchester, and died in Borrowdale in 1851 at the age of 72, leaving a son and daughter.

Thomas Hayton and Richard Bowness, the stonemasons who built the bridge, lived in Keswick.

Forestry Commission Monument - Whinlatter

Inscription

Erected to Commemorate
The Jubilee of
The
FORESTRY COMMISSION
1919 - 1969
The first plantations begun by the Governors of Greenwich Hospital and Thomas Story c.1790 extended by John Marshall 1848 Felled to meet the Nation's Needs 1914 -1918. The first trees replanted by the Forestry Commissioners at Hospital Plantation 9th December,1919
From this grew
THORNTHWAITE FOREST

O.S. Map: English Lakes NW 1:25000   **Grid ref:** 224245
Grade: C
Location
   Leaving Braithwaite village near Keswick, Whinlatter Pass climbs steeply to a viewpoint and parking area on the right, immediately opposite the Forestry Commission's car park at Noble Knott.

A short distance down Whinlatter Pass from the car park is a sign 'Brows Wood'. Go through the gap in the wall by the sign, turn right and you will see the monument under the trees.

Information

When James Radcliffe, the third Earl of Derwentwater, was executed in 1716 for supporting the Jacobite Rebellion of 1715, his property around Keswick, which included Whinlatter and Thornthwaite, was given to the Governors of Greenwich Hospital, who took an interest in their northern estate and began to stock the woods with conifers. They introduced European Larch, which years later Wordsworth scathingly dismissed as 'a sort of vegetable manufactury'. But John Marshall, a friend of the poet, recognised the value of conifers and, when he acquired the Greenwich Hospital estate in 1832, he set about planting a large area of Whinlatter with Norway Spruce. All these pioneer plantations were felled during the 1914-18 war when imports of timber into the UK were cut off, and in 1919 the Government set up the Forestry Commission with a directive to rebuild a strategic reserve of timber. The Commission acquired much of the old Greenwich Hospital estate, and Thornthwaite failed by only one day to go down in history as the oldest of the Commission's forests. The first trees were planted near the summit of Whinlatter Pass on the 9th of December 1919, a day after the Commission's very first trees were planted at Eggesford, in Devon. At least, that's the official version of events. According to the forestry workers employed at the time, determined that Thornthwaite would claim the honour of planting the first trees, the men held their own unofficial tree-planting ceremony at Whinlatter on December 7th. If only someone had taken a photograph and had it witnessed!

On Monday the 9th of June 1969, to mark the Jubilee of the Forestry Commission, an attractive cone-shaped local stone cairn was unveiled in Brows Wood by Leslie Jenkins, the Chairman of the Forestry Commission and, commenting on the superb panoramic view from the site, he said it was evidence that forestry can be productive without being unlovely.

Gough's Monument - Helvellyn

Inscription

Beneath this spot were found in 1805 the remains of Charles Gough Killed by a fall from the rocks, his dog was still guarding the skeleton.   Walter Scott describes the event in the poem 'I climbed the dark brow of the mighty Helvellyn'. Wordsworth records it in his lines on Fidelity which conclude with:-

> The dog which still was hovering nigh
> Repeating the same timid cry
> This dog had been through three months space
> A dweller in that savage place
>
> How nourished here through such long time
> He knows who gave that love sublime
> And gave that strength of feeling great
> Above all human estimate.
> In memory of that love & strength of feeling
> This stone is erected
>   FPC   1890   HDR

O.S. Map: English Lakes NE 1:25000   **Grid ref:** 344151

57

Grade: A

Location

A short distance SE of Helvellyn Summit, immediately above Striding Edge. Marked as 'Monument' on O.S. map

Information

"On the Eighteenth Day of the Fourth Month called April, one thousand seven hundred and eighty-two was born at Manchester, in the Parish of Manchester, in the County of Lancaster, unto Joseph Gough, junr., and Margaret his wife, a son, who was named Charles". The son of a well-to-do Quaker family, young Charles was an accomplished artist and a keen naturalist and angler who spent all his spare time in the Lake District. He was a well-known figure in Patterdale and at the now long-demolished Cherry Tree Inn at Wythburn where, according to the locals, "He knew ivery beck this side o' t' Raise." On the morning of the 18th of April 1805, accompanied by his little Irish terrier and carrying a few clothes and his fishing rod, he set off from Patterdale to cross Helvellyn and spend a few days at the Cherry Tree Inn. It was his twenty third birthday and, although there was snow on the fell tops and a blustery wind driving showers of sleet across the valleys, he probably felt on top of the world. Ignoring warnings that it was unwise to venture on high ground, he set off on the path for Striding Edge and was never seen alive again.

Fourteen weeks later, on Saturday the 20th of July, a Patterdale shepherd was gathering sheep near Red Tarn, below the summit of Helvellyn, when he made a bizarre discovery. Attracted by the barking of a dog, he found a little terrier standing guard over a headless human skeleton, later identified as the remains of Charles Gough. It sparked off endless speculation about how the body came to be lying where it was found, but local opinion favoured the theory that he had fallen off the end of Striding Edge, or from the rock buttresses close by, immediately below the summit of Helvellyn. His skull was later retrieved and the remains buried in a Quaker grave-yard near Penrith. That none of his family seems to have made enquiries about his whereabouts during the three months he was missing could perhaps be accounted for by the fact that he had been disowned by the Quakers for joining the army Volunteers.

The discovery of Gough's headless skeleton, still clothed and near to the remains of his fishing rod, notebook, watch, hat and a lock of his hair, would have been the main topic of conversation in the houses and inns of Patterdale for months, but what really captured the heart of the nation and inspired poets and artists was the incredible story of how Gough's little terrier bitch had stayed by his body. In fact, not only had it stayed by the body but it had given birth to a pup or pups - accounts differ about how many - though none had survived.

To the people and the poets the terrier was a heroine and they were outraged when a newspaper printed a sensational story about how the dog was found near its master's remains 'uncommonly fat and the flesh of the latter mostly consumed'. All sorts of theories were put forward about how the dog had survived, and the suggestion that the starving terrier had chewed through poor Gough's remains was angrily denounced. The newspaper journalist responsible for the report quickly responded with, 'In contradiction of the report that the dog had eaten his master, I have to state, from the opinion of some well-informed people in the neighbourhood, that from the frequency of the carcases of animals being devoured by birds of prey, there can be little doubt that his body had fallen a sacrifice to those voracious birds.'

Gough's body would undoubtedly have attracted scavenging birds, and even foxes and other mammals; but though the newspaper's first article caused great offence amongst its readers, probably because the reality was too ghastly to contemplate, there were many who believed strongly that a starving dog, however loyal to its master, was unlikely to have ignored titbits scattered about by the scavengers.

In his book 'Past and Present at the Lakes', Canon Rawnsley devotes a whole chapter to Gough and his dog, and it is the most reasoned account of the tragedy to be found. It was Canon Rawnsley, with a friend, Miss Frances Power Cobbe, who paid for the monument to Gough on Helvellyn summit; "a stone that may, with its simple tale, touch the hearts of passers-by for generations to come, and stand a monument to heroic vigil, and to the fidelity and love, no death could quench, of the humble 'Friend of Man'." The date on the monument is 1890 but, according to Rawnsley, it was erected on the 18th of June 1891.

Hallworth's Bridge - Stonethwaite

Inscription

This bridge was re-erected in memory of Gordon Hallworth, aged 21 years a devoted member of the M/UNIV MTG. CLUB who during the night following 7th January 1939 died of exhaustion in this Dale notwithstanding the self-sacrificing assistance of his two companions and the strenuous efforts of a relief party of their friends. May 1939

O.S. Map: English Lakes NW 1:25000   **Grid ref:** 274130
Grade: C
Location
Smithymire Island - 1 mile up Greenup Gill from Stonethwaite, Borrowdale
Information
The Whitehaven News of 12th January 1939 reported:-
'A Manchester physics student, Gordon F. Hallworth, B.Sc., 21 years of age, whose home was at Hale, Cheshire, died on the Lakeland hills in the early hours of Sunday morning from exhaustion, due to exposure. He was one of a party of 19 members of Manchester University Mountaineering Club who were staying

in the Lake District during the week-end. About noon on Saturday, he left Rosthwaite, along with Michael Boyle and Douglas Boyle, brothers, to climb over Glaramara and Allen Crag to Esk Hause and return by Langstrath. They were apparently unaware that the bridge over Langstrath Beck, which was shown on the map, had been washed away some years ago, for they made for this point to cross the beck.

An accident, putting their electric torch out of use, prevented them consulting their map again, as it was then dark, and unaware that there were bridges within a comparatively short distance, they began to climb Green Gill to find a ford. During this journey both Hallworth and Michael Boyle became exhausted, and Douglas Boyle went to find a rescue party. He was unable to get anyone until he reached Rosthwaite, and when the party reached Hallworth he was dead. Michael Boyle recovered after attention.

Douglas S. Boyle, medical student at Manchester University, son of Dr. Boyle, Disley, Cheshire, told how they set out for a climb at noon on Saturday, and planned to be back about half-past five to six. All went nicely until about half-past five, when they arrived at the junction of Greenup Gill at the bottom of Langstrath, the bridge there had been washed away, and unfortunately they had missed the other bridge. They reclimbed the fell. It was dark, and by this time they were, not unnaturally, tired. About half-way up the fell, when they were level with Eagle Crag, Hallworth showed signs of distress, and witness's brother, Michael, had to support him, and then both of them had to support Hallworth with their arms around him. At one point they had to carry him. They sat down frequently, but when they did so they got cold, and had to put their arms round one another to keep warm. The beck was in spate and they could not cross it, but, with some difficulty, his brother Michael got across with the aid of a long pole, which, witness held set against the bank. Hallworth was assisted across with the poles but fell in, and Michael had to get him out of the water and on to the bank.

As they descended the fell on the far side of the Gill, Hallworth suggested many times that they should leave him as he was holding them back. They tried to cheer him by talking about the dinner they would have when they got back to Rosthwaite. They had food with them. His brother, Michael, began to fall with Hallworth as he

61

assisted him, and then all three of them began to fall together. Finally Hallworth could not walk, as his legs were so weak, and when they were about level with Eagle Crag on the far side of the Gill witness managed to get Hallworth in behind a boulder, and they made him as comfortable as possible. He thought the best thing to do was to hurry down as soon as possible. Then his brother collapsed. Witness hurried down to Stonethwaite, but could not make anyone hear at the two or three doors at which he knocked. He hurried on to Rosthwaite, and arrived there about 1.30 a.m. He went back with rescue party at once. They found his brother and sent him back in a car and went on to Hallworth.

Dr. Alec Martin, Dalton Hall, Manchester, one of the rescue party, said that Hallworth died from heart failure due to exhaustion and exposure to cold.'

Hamer Memorials - Borrowdale
John Hamer Memorial

Inscription

Castle Crag was given to the
National Trust in memory of
JOHN HAMER
2nd Lieut 6th KSLI Born July 8 1897
Killed in action March 22 1918
Also of
The following men of Borrowdale
Who died for the same cause
2nd Lieut H.E. Layland R.E.

Pte G. Bird	1st	Border Regt
Pte E.J. Boow	2nd	Border Regt
Pte J.H. Dover	11th	Border Regt
Pte J. Edmondson	1st	Border Regt
Pte F. Hindmoor	7th	Border Regt
Pte W. Nicholson	5th	Border Regt
Pte T. Richardson	6th	Border Regt
Pte J.W. Rigg	8th	Border Regt
Pte A.E. Wilson		Kings Own Royal Lancasters

O.S. Map: English Lakes NW 1:25000   **Grid ref:** 249159
Grade: C
Location

On the Grange to Seatoller bridleway in Borrowdale, about 1 mile south of Grange, a thin path leaves the bridleway on the left hand side and ascends through a gap in a wall on a zigzag course which eventually reaches the summit of Castle Crag. A fine place from which to enjoy the rugged beauty of the Borrowdale valley. The memorial is attached to a small rocky outcrop on the summit.

Information

Although the Hamer family, who lived in London, do not appear to have owned any land or property in the Lake District, they obviously had a great love for Borrowdale and the view from Castle Crag. Probably persuaded by Samuel Hamer, the brother of Sir William and the Secretary of the National Trust from 1911 to 1933, Sir William and Lady Hamer made a donation to the National Trust in 1918 to buy land as a memorial to their son, 21 year old John Hamer, who was killed in France in March 1918. In 1920 eighteen acres at the top of Castle Crag were purchased for £150 from the Executors of Colonel C.V. Conway Gordon, and handed over to the National Trust. It was the intention of the Hamers that the plaque fixed to a rock on the summit be solely to the memory of John Hamer but they were persuaded by Canon Rawnsley to add the names of the men of Borrowdale who had fallen in the war, even though there was already a memorial to them in Grange churchyard.

Sir William Hamer's Plaque and Agnes Hamer's Seat

Inscription
The land surrounding the summit of Castle Crag was given to the Nation in memory of Sir William Hamer M.A. M.D. F.R.C.P. by his wife Agnes, whom this seat commemorates. 1939

O.S. Map: English Lakes NW 1:25000   **Grid ref:** 248158
Location
A short distance along the path leading up Castle Crag, a thin path branches right and climbs easily to a rocky ledge where there is a wooden seat and a plaque overhung by a Yew tree.
Information
Sir William Heaton Hamer was an eminent doctor who specialised in the study of epidemics. Having spent some time as a lecturer on the subject at St Bartholomew's Hospital, he was later for many years the Medical Officer of Health and School Medical Officer for London. In 1923 he was knighted for his contribution to medicine. When he died in 1938 his brother Samuel, on behalf of Lady Hamer, asked William Heelis, the husband of Beatrix Potter, to enquire about the possibility of acquiring the lower slopes of Castle Crag, and in due course the 23 acre Low Hows Wood was given to the National Trust in memory of Sir William. The generosity of the Hamer family has enabled many thousands of visitors to enjoy exploring a very striking feature in the landscape of Borrowdale.

Harry Kirkby's Memorial - Ennerdale

Inscription

Dedicated to Harry Kirkby died 1996
For his outstanding contributions to
hound trailing

O.S. Map: English lakes NW 1:25000   **Grid ref:** 089185
Grade: C

Location

Ennerdale Show Field, The Leaps. 1 mile east of Kirkland, the Kirkland to Croasdale road meets a T junction. Turn left and descend the hill to where the embankment of an old mine railway can be seen on the right. A stile gives access to the top of the embankment and below on the right is a field flanked by a long stone wall. The plaque will be found built into the wall.

Note: The top of the embankment is a permissive path but the field below it is not. Access to the plaque is due to the goodwill of the landowner. Please do not climb the wall or fences, and keep away from grazing stock.

Information

Some people confuse hound trailing with fox hunting but, despite the name, hound trailing has no connection whatsoever with hunting. Wealthy arabs and business tycoons may consider horse racing to be the Sport of Kings, but in West Cumbria the King of Sports is hound trailing. It is essentially a dog race in which specially bred and incredibly well-cared-for hounds, fed on a diet of best steak and milk stout, compete against each other in a race over the fells. Someone once said that compared with experiencing the joy of the setting amongst the lakes and fells, the thrill of seeing the hounds streaking across a hillside, clearing the drystone walls and gates in a single jump, and witnessing the frenzy of the finish with the whistles and shouts of the owners urging their dogs to the line, horse racing was about as exciting as watching a line of rabbits chasing each other along a railway embankment.

At hound trailing events there are no gents in morning suits or ladies in outrageous hats but, as in all sports involving competitors with four legs, competition between owners is very fierce and placing bets with a bookmaker very popular. To ensure that everything is well organised and scrupulously fair, the ruling body of the sport, the Hound Trailing Association, appoints officials who have had a lifetime association with the sport and who are highly respected. Such a man was Henry (Harry) Kirkby of Arlecdon.

Harry was born at Wath Brow, near Cleator Moor, in 1927, and when he was a boy he used to earn pocket money 'walking out' hounds belonging to Mrs Foy, a well-known breeder of trail hounds at that time. Fired by Mrs Foy's enthusiasm, and having learnt a few tricks of the trade from her, Harry was eventually elected onto the hound trailing committee of Cleator Moor Celtic football team who ran hound trails to raise funds. He was slightly built and not very tall, but what he lacked in stature he made up in determination and courage. 'La'al Harry' was renowned for being very strict and sticking to the rules, even when confronted by someone twice his size who angrily disagreed with his decision. But though some resented his firmness, his knowledge of hounds and hound trailing made him widely respected and he was much in demand as a committee member and as a judge at events all over Cumbria and the Borders.

It was said that in the hound trailing season, from April to October, Harry never missed an event; no matter how far he had to travel and despite being employed on shift work at the Marchon chemical company in Whitehaven. Apparently he had very accommodating workmates who swopped shifts with him. Harry's almost fanatical enthusiasm for hound trailing earned him the title of 'Mr Hound Trailing' and he was elected Chairman of Whitehaven Area Branch of the Hound Trailing Association, and Vice Chairman of both the Hound Trailing Association and the International Hound Trailing Association. In 1994 his contribution to the sport was further recognised when the Whitehaven Area committee presented him with a plaque honouring his 'outstanding and dedicated service to hound trailing.'

For many years Harry organised hound trailing events at Ennerdale Show, now located in the Leaps, a field near Ennerdale owned by a local farmer, Mr Peter Mitchell; and when Harry died after a long illness in February 1996, his ashes were scattered over the field. In Harry's memory, the Whitehaven Area committee awarded a challenge cup and also wished to erect a memorial plaque. It so happened that every year at Ennerdale Show the National Trust's Wardens, with Peter Mitchell's permission, took down part of the field wall and rebuilt it again to demonstrate to visitors the art of dry stone wall building. The Wardens readily agreed to build the memorial plaque to Harry Kirkby into the wall during the 1996 Show, and it is there for all to see.

Hodgson's Well - Borrowdale

Inscription

Memoriam
W. Hodgson
He prayeth well who loved well
Both man and bird and beast

For the dear God who loveth us He made and loveth all
SEPTEMBER
1878

O.S. Map: English Lakes NW 1:25000   **Grid ref:** 254171
Grade: C
Location
On the left hand side of a bend in the road, half a mile south of Grange in Borrowdale, heading for Rosthwaite. Keep a sharp look out for a very attractive little stone monument and water trough which, in summer, is ablaze with wild flowers.

Information

William Hodgson is one of the Lake District's 'forgotten artists' and a rather melancholy report about him appeared in the West Cumberland Times of 21 September 1878 :-

'A young artist of great promise succumbed to a lingering disease on Wednesday last at Keswick, where he resided with his parents, at the early age of 18. He was of an amiable disposition and universally loved by all who knew him. In him art has lost one who bade fair to take the highest position in that noble and elevating profession. He studied for some time at the Lambeth School of Art in London where his talents were so well recognised that the Master, Mr Sparks, tried to induce him to remain for the Lambeth School was famed for having trained some of the cleverest young artists of the day and could ill afford to lose such a clever pupil. His works at the Keswick School of Art where he studied so assiduously since its opening received the highest amount of money reward to the school from the Government. He executed many works in oil and watercolour of great excellence for one so young...his most important picture being "Daniel in the Den of Lions" painted in the winter of last year. We fear that over assiduity to excel in his art may have led to too close an application to study which acted injuriously on a constitution not naturally strong.'

William Hodgson's parents erected the monument in his memory.

Horse Monument - Thirlmere

Inscription

30th   9 mo   1843
Fallen from his fellows side,
The steed beneath is lying,
In harness, here, he died,
His only fault was dying.
WB

(The initials WB stood for W Ball, a local poet)

O.S. Map: English Lakes NE 1:25000   **Grid ref:** 325124
Grade: C - but note the warning

Location

Passed within inches by hundreds of cars, coaches and lorries, this memorial tablet is set into a roadside wall adjacent to the bridge over Birkside Gill, about 1 mile north of Dunmail Raise on the A591 Grasmere-Keswick road. Coming from Keswick, it is about 300 yards beyond the Armboth junction at the south end of Thirlmere.

Warning. The posterior of the person bending to read the inscription protrudes onto this very busy road, a hazard to speeding motorists not allowed for on any of the road signs!

Information

The rather touching inscription records the death of one of the horses that pulled the passenger and mail coach which used to run between Ambleside and Keswick. One of the stopping places was the Nags Head Inn at Wythburn. It was immediately opposite Wythburn church but was demolished when Manchester Corporation moved the road prior to raising the level of Thirlmere.

Few of the coach horses survived the 1914-1918 war, and the introduction of the motor charabanc in 1919 heralded the end of horse-drawn passenger transport in the Lakes. The last horse-drawn coach along Thirlmere side ran in 1926. No more did the drivers shout "First class sit still! Second class, walk! Third class, shuv!" when the coach reached the foot of the climb up Dunmail Raise.

Fortunately Manchester Corporation Waterworks preserved this relic of Lakeland coaching era by building it into a wall when the road was widened in 1948. It would have been more accessible had it been built into a cairn at Wythburn church, but how could the authority have anticipated that, fifty years on, in excess of 12 million people would be descending on the Lake District during the tourist season, and the road would be so busy with traffic that trying to read the stone tablet would be extremely hazardous.

There is another version of the story about the monument in a guide to the Lakes counties published in the 1930s:-

"Along the old coach road over the pass William Ball drove every Sunday from Rydal to the little Friends Meeting House at Colthouse. One of his horses fell dead in harness, and in harness it was buried where a stone in the wall of the old road, near the top of the Raise bears the inscription Mr Ball wrote in memory of his faithful friend, whose only fault was dying." The story might be credible were it not that Rydal and Colthouse, near Hawkshead, are on the south side of the pass (Dunmail Raise) whereas the monument is on the north side and completely in the opposite direction if travelling from Rydal to Colthouse.

Hugh Walpole's Seat and Plaque - Derwentwater

Inscription

To the memory of Sir Hugh Walpole C.B.E. of Brackenburn
This seat is erected by his friend Harold Cheevers
September 1941

Also on plaque above the garage of Brackenburn Lodge:-

Hugh Walpole, Novelist lived and wrote here 1924-1941

O.S. Map: English Lakes NW 1:25000   **Grid ref:** 248193
Grade: C
Location
   On the Portinscale to Grange-in-Borrowdale road. The seat
is immediately above Brackenburn house on the public bridleway
between Manesty and Hawse End. Easy access from Manesty, or
go past Brackenburn to a good parking area and access to the
bridleway by Brandlehow Wood.
Note: Brackenburn and Brackenburn Lodge are private houses.
Please respect the privacy of the owners.

Information

Hugh Walpole is best known for his Herries novels, set in Borrowdale, viz: Rogue Herries, Judith Paris, The Fortress and Vanessa. He was born in Auckland, New Zealand, where his father was a Canon in St Mary's Cathedral. When Walpole senior later returned to the UK - at various times he was Principal of Bede College, Durham and Bishop of Edinburgh - Hugh was educated at King's School, Canterbury and at Cambridge University. While at university he wrote two novels, one of which he destroyed, but the other was published five years later as his first book, though it barely recovered the cost of having the manuscript typed. However, he was a prolific writer and success soon came his way. He was said to have written a book a year from the publication of his first novel in his youth to his death in 1941. One critic wrote of him, 'Just when a reader becomes convinced that Hugh Walpole is a feathery, confiding, complacent man of letters, he begins to write like a great writer; and just when the reader becomes convinced that he is a great writer, he begins to write like a feathery, confiding, complacent man of letters'. He wrote several plays which were performed on stage, and also made a film version of David Copperfield.

During the 1914-18 war he served with the Red Cross in Russia and was decorated for his heroism in rescuing a wounded man under fire. After the war he lived in London and, as a director of the English Book Society, he travelled regularly to the the United States. He was made a CBE in 1918 , and knighted in 1937.

Walpole was described as 'a big man, handsome in his youth, later completely bald and spectacled but still impressive with his square head and massive dome forehead'. He never married, and divided his time between a flat in London and his country home at Brackenburn, 'where he could retreat and be alone with his dogs and his books'. He was an authority on Sir Walter Scott and owned the world's finest collection of Scott manuscripts and memorabilia.

Sir Hugh Walpole was a well-known figure in Borrowdale and Keswick, and died of a heart attack through over-exertion during a 'War Weapons Week' parade in Keswick in 1941. He was 57.

John Bankes Esq - Seathwaite

Inscription

Stone No 1

John Bankes Esqre
This stone replaces an
exactly similar stone
wilfully destroyed
November 1887
Replaced by the
National Trust 1983

O.S. Map: English Lakes NW 1:2500   **Grid ref:** 233126

Grade: B

Location

Take the path for Sour Milk Gill from Seathwaite farm, Borrowdale, and, having crossed the wooden bridge over the river, immediately turn right and pick up a path heading through the ruins of old mine workings to a gate in the wall. Take care not to walk on Stone No 1, lying in the grass as you approach the gate. Continue on through the gate and along the riverside path to where Newhouse Gill discharges into the river. Follow the right hand bank of Newhouse Gill until a path can be picked up which zigzags steeply up the fell side to the wad mine workings. Another stone inscribed 'John Bankes Esqre' will be found by the side of the path on the way up, but the date has been obliterated by vandals. Altogether five stones were placed around the mine to mark the boundary; but, though we have searched on several occasions, we have not been able to locate all of them.

Information

Black lead - known officially as plumbago and locally as wad, was mined at Seathwaite for many centuries and was the foundation of the Cumberland pencil industry which still survives in Keswick. Borrowdale Wad was considered to be the purest in the world, and Robinson's Natural History of Westmorland & Cumberland states:-

"Its natural uses are both medicinal and mechanical. It is a present remedy for cholic; it easeth the pain of gravel, stone and strangury: and, for these and like uses, it is much bought up by apothecaries and physicians. The manner of the country people using it is thus: first they beat it small into meal, and then take as much of it, in white wine or ale, as will lie upon a sixpence, or more, if the distemper requires it. It operates by urine, sweat and vomiting.....it is bought up at high prices by the Hollanders and others. Besides medicinal it has many uses...... it was used by the neighbourhood at first only for marking their sheep but now used to glaze and harden crucibles and other vessels made of earth or clay, that are to endure the hottest fire, and to that end is wonderfully effectual.. By rubbing it upon iron arms, as guns, pistols, and the like, and tinging them with its colour, it preserves them from rusting."

Seathwaite wad mine was acquired by Sir John Bankes in 1622. Born in Keswick in 1589, he qualified as a lawyer in London, and with high prices being paid for wad he obviously saw it as a good investment. At the height of the demand for wad it was so valuable the mine was regularly attacked by robbers, who hid their loot in a stone hut perched on a ledge on the Ennerdale side of Great Gable. Armed guards patrolled the mine day and night, but the attacks continued and an Act of Parliament was passed which made the theft of wad, or even trespass on the mine, an offence punishable by a public flogging, twelve months hard labour, or seven years deportation. To mark the boundary of his mine, Sir John Bankes had five large pieces of slate engraved with his name, or that of his partner Mr Shepherd, and fixed at various locations.

The mine operated for many years under various owners, but the demand for wad steadily declined, and it finally closed in 1891.

John Litt's Monument - Thirlmere

Inscription - two stone pillars

North pillar:-   In memory of J.Litt 1880
South pillar:-

We found this stone in Mere Gill that steep and beautiful mountain Rill. To mark the Spot where his Spirit fled to the Glorious home where no tears are shed.

O.S. Map: English Lakes NW 1:25000   **Grid ref:** 293185
Grade: A
Location
   Mere Gill, Thirlmere. The usual approach to Litt's Monument is from Shoulthwaite Farm, about 3 miles south of Keswick on the A 591. When through the farm yard into the wood, keep a sharp lookout for a path on the right which climbs up through the wood to a forest road. Turn right on the forest road, and follow until a wooden bridge can be seen on the right spanning Shoulthwaite Gill. Over the bridge, turn left and follow a narrow path below the massive rock buttress of Iron Crag until it crosses Mere Gill. Climb the right hand side of Mere Gill until, high up, the angle eases and the gill can be crossed. Climb the little knoll ahead and the two pillars will come in sight.
Note: Approaching Mere Gill the path is exposed, and the climb up Mere Gill can be taxing. For experienced walkers only.
For an easier but longer route, requiring a map and clear visibility -

do not cross the wooden bridge over Soulthwaite Gill but continue on up the forest road to its summit where a gate in the deer fence gives access to the open fell. Make for the prominent summit of High Seat and descend the easy grassy slope to the top of Mere Gill and Litt's Monument

Information

That there are two stone pillars, one beautifully inscribed with a touching poem, gives the impression that it is a memorial to one of the local landed gentry; but a report in the West Cumberland Times for the 13th of March 1880 reveals the story of an ordinary chap who obviously had many friends:-

'On Tuesday or Wednesday last Mr John Litt, omnibus driver, aged 48 years, died very suddenly. It appears that on Tuesday morning the deceased went out to take part in a hunt at Castlerigg Fell, and did not return home after the hunt was over, or during the night. On the following morning this was communicated to his uncle, Mr John Keenliside, by the deceased's wife. Mr Keenliside at once made inquiries concerning him, and ascertaining where he had last been seen, organised a search party and immediately went in search of the missing man. Thomas Hudspith and a man named Oliver, on Tuesday morning, at half-past ten o' clock, had left Mr Litt sitting on Knowe Crag; and Oliver, with another man named David Pooley proceeded to the place, where they discovered the deceased a short distance from the spot where he had previously been observed. He was lying on his back and it seemed as if he had fallen. In the meantime a number of the search party appeared on the scene, and the body of Mr Litt was borne away. Subsequently they came across a cart into which the body was placed and conveyed to Keswick, which place was reached at about three o' clock, the body being found at about eleven o' clock in the morning. Dr O' Reilly certified that the cause of death was heart disease. The deceased leaves a wife and two children.'

King Edward V11 Monument - Borrowdale

Inscription

In loving memory of King Edward V11 Grange Fell is dedicated by his sister Louise as a sanctuary of rest and peace.

Here may all beings gather strength
Find in scenes of beautiful nature a cause
For gratitude and love to God giving them
Courage and vigour to carry on his will.

O.S. Map: English Lakes NW 1:2500   **Grid ref:** 258167

Grade: B

Location

One of the most popular approaches to Grange Fell starts at a stile next to Grange View house, a few yards south of Grange Bridge, in Borrowdale. From the stile, the path climbs through a delightful wood to a gate in a wall. Beyond the gate the main path sweeps left and heads down Troutdale, but a right fork climbs steeply up the left side of Great End Crag. The ascent is made easier, though somewhat tedious, by a magnificent stone staircase built by the National Trust. The plaque is on a heather-draped rock face below the north side of the summit. A magnificent view of Grange and Derwentwater from the top.

Information

In a letter to the West Cumberland Times of the 17th of August 1910, Canon Rawnsley, the honorary secretary, and Mr Nigel Bond, the secretary of the National Trust, wrote:

'It has been the idea of the founders of the National Trust from the beginning that gifts to the nation of places of beauty or of historic interest would form very fit memorials of those who have passed away. It is with great pleasure that we announce that our President, the Princess Louise, has determined to purchase the superb view-point of Grange Fell, in Borrowdale and make it, through the National Trust, a gift to the public in memory of the late King. We shall thus have the name of Edward VII permanently connected with the Lake District, and, as Victoria Bay on Derwentwater preserves the name of his mother, so King Edward's Fell in Borrowdale will preserve the name of her honoured son.

There are still several acres of the fell that can be added to the memorial if friends desire to do so. An acre costs £7 7s. We have raised £1,650; there remains £750 to be obtained before the purchase can be completed. 'Ignotus,' as you kindly allowed us to intimate in your columns, has offered £100 towards the purchase of the Borrowdale property on condition that nine others will give a like sum. Two of these donors - one of them our President - have responded to this appeal.'

The balance was soon raised by public subscription and Grange Fell, which included Bowderstone Cottage and the well-known tourist attraction, the Bowderstone, estimated to weigh over 2,000 tonnes, became the property of the Nation. A fine memorial to King Edward, and one that was more in keeping with his title of 'Edward the Peacemaker' than the insensitive proposal from the Chairman and Secretary of the 'Universal Service Petition' -that the people should 'adopt a Universal Military Service in memory of King Edward, and in so doing we shall prove our loyalty to King George.'

Malkinson's Monument - Eskdale

Inscription

In Memory of
William Malkinson
Wesleyan Local Preacher
Died here suddenly
Sunday Feb 21 1886
Be Ye Also Ready

O.S. Map: English Lakes SW 1:25000   **Grid ref:** 17014
Grade: C
Location
   By the roadside, on the left, where the Gosforth-Eskdale road
levels out having climbed steeply from Santon Bridge.
Information
   The morning of Sunday the 21st of February 1886 was bitterly
cold, and thick fog had descended from Irton Pike and drifted down

into Eskdale and Santon Bridge, reducing visibility to a few yards. It was a day when most folk would have been content to stay by their fireside; but 54 year old William Malkinson, Clerk and Surveyor to the Cleator Moor Local Board and a lay preacher for many years, had been invited to take the service at the Wesleyan Chapel in Eskdale. He had a reputation for never letting a congregation down, and by numerous lifts on horse-drawn carts had made the long journey from Cleator Moor; and called at the house of a Wesleyan, Joseph Huddart, in Santon Bridge, for a rest before walking with him to Eskdale. Over a cup of coffee, William Malkinson mentioned that he suffered from asthma and had difficulty in breathing, and when the pair eventually set off up the steep hill out of Santon Bridge they agreed not to talk. William Malkinson walked on one side of the road and Joseph Huddart on the other. They were only half way up the hill when Malkinson began to show signs of exertion and, gasping for breath, said he would have to slow down. Huddart joked, "We'll take a reef in the sail," and the pace was slackened but, as they neared the top of the hill, Malkinson suddenly gave a moan and collapsed onto the grass verge. Joseph Huddart tore off his necktie and collar and tried to revive him, but there was no sign of life.

At the inquest at the Santon Bridge Hotel, Dr Parker of Gosforth said that William Malkinson had died from heart failure; but added, "He had on two waistcoats, two coats and two mufflers; in fact he had on sufficient clothes to embarrass and make the breathing more difficult, even on level ground. He had on too much, especially walking up such a hill as he was going up."

William Malkinson's friends, and members of the Wesleyan Church, subscribed to have a stone monument erected on the spot where he fell.

Maria Loechle's Cross - Buttermere

Inscription

In Memory of Maria Antonia Loechle
accidentally killed 9 April 1963

O.S. Map: English Lakes NW 1:25000   **Grid ref:** 217147
Grade: C - but see caution

Location

Approaching Honister Pass from Gatesgarth, Buttermere, the road crosses Gatesgarthdale beck by a prominent bridge. Over the bridge, keep a sharp lookout for a stone sheep fold on the left. From the sheep fold strike up towards a solitary tree on a narrow grassy rib. Continue up the grass rib to where it joins scree. Climb the scree to the foot of the crag immediately ahead, and look for the small oak cross tucked in at the base of the rock. It is not easy to see against the dark rock.

Caution - The approach needs care. The angle of the grass and the scree is steeper than it looks from the road.

Information

On the 7th of April 1963 two young German girls, Maria Antonia Loechle (Toni) and Gudrun Strobel, both from Memmingham in

West Germany, arrived in Keswick at the start of a walking holiday. Both had been working as 'au pairs' with families in north Lancashire, and were eagerly looking forward to exploring the Lake District.

They left Keswick about 11.30 a.m. on Tuesday the 9th, and walked up Catbells and along Maiden Moor until they reached Dalehead Tarn. From there they intended to follow the track to Buttermere marked on the map by Dalehead, Hindscarth Edge, Littledale Edge and Robinson; but on Dalehead they became confused in misty conditions and when, through a break in the mist, they saw a river and a road in the valley below, they decided to head down the mountain. It was a fateful decision. Unaware of the danger, they started to descend the near-vertical crags on the north side of Honister Pass. The mists swirled around them reducing visibility to a few yards and, as the angle of the rock steepened, they were soon in difficulty and found themselves unable to climb up or down. While Toni Loechle was desperately searching for a way down, Gudrun heard her cry out through the mist, then seconds later heard a crash as she hit the screes far below, then silence. Though shocked and terrified, Gudrun realised that she had to be extra careful; but, while attempting to get round a large rock, she slipped and plunged down the crag. "I went round and round and shut my eyes and hit a stone and hurt myself. I lay there for a bit. I still knew about it. I could not walk properly. I sat down and let myself slide."

By a stroke of luck she had landed on the scree slope below the crag and slid down a considerable distance; and though she suffered head injuries, the steep angle of the scree probably saved her life. In considerable pain, she managed to slide down the scree and reach the road where, fortunately, a car stopped and took her to Gatesgarth.

Sadly, 23 year old Toni Loechle was killed instantly by the fall. She was taken back to Germany.

Someone, perhaps one of her family, has placed a small oak cross at the foot of the crag where she fell.

Mountain Rescue Memorial - Buttermere

Inscription

John C Thomson
Age 49 killed 15th June 1969
and
Michael Stephenson
Age 28 died 16th June 1969
Who gave their lives in
service for others
during a Mountain Rescue practice

O.S. Map: English Lakes NW 1:25000 **Grid ref:** 186148
Grade: C
Location
   From Gatesgarth Farm, Buttermere, follow the path for Scarth Gap
Pass to a footbridge and a gate. Through the gate a path turns sharp
right for Burtness Wood, but ignore it and climb a short distance up
the Scarth Gap Pass until a path forks right heading for Burtness
Combe. A few minutes walk and Low Crag and the plaque will be
seen on the left.

Information

The majority of walkers taking the path from Gatesgarth to Burtness Combe and High Stile probably pass by the unassuming outcrop of Low Crag without giving it a second glance. But on the 15th of June 1969 it was the scene of one of the worst tragedies in the history of British Mountain Rescue when two of the most experienced members of Cockermouth Mountain Rescue Team died as a result of a rock-fall while they were involved in a stretcher lowering practice.

The West Cumberland Times & Star of the 21st of June reported:-

' Mr John C. Thomson, of Mayo Street, Cockermouth, 46-year-old head of the English department at Derwent School, Cockermouth, died instantly.

Mr Michael Stephenson, aged 27, of Briar Bank, Cockermouth, a draughtsman at Distington Engineering Co., Workington, died from his injuries the following day in West Cumberland Hospital.

It is understood that part of the rock face, which had been used as a belay point for similar practices on previous occasions, came away.

The fall was seen by Mr Thomas Richardson, of Gatesgarth Farm, who was watching the practice from his farmyard. Soon afterwards one of the team ran across the fields to give the alarm.

Mr Richardson contacted a lady doctor who was on holiday at the Bridge Hotel, Buttermere, and she helped the injured until they could be removed to hospital. Keswick Mountain Rescue Team was called out to assist.

Still in hospital as a result of the accident is Miss Katherine Walton, an instructor at Sunderland Education Committee's outdoor pursuits centre at Portinscale. The other casualties were Mr John Derek Daley, of Slatefell Avenue, Cockermouth, who had superficial injuries, Mr Keith Lister, of Briar Bank, Cockermouth, who had rope-burns to his hands, Mr James Andrew Coyle of Dalton Street, Cockermouth, (a fractured radius) and Mr Rex Usher, of Albemarle Street, Cockermouth, who was severely bruised. Mr Usher, who is also a teacher at Derwent School, was strapped into a stretcher for an exercise rescue, and was being lowered down a face crag on Low Crag, across the valley from Gatesgarth farm.

At Thursday's service, the Vicar of Cockermouth, the Ven. W E A Pugh, said that in this part of the world we were all too familiar with accidents to people who through ignorance or carelessness ventured onto the fells, but this was not such a case. "Here we had a group of people who knew their mountains, men of skill and experience who were not out on a Sunday just for enjoyment but to improve their skill so that at times when others got into difficulties they might be able to help them. Tragedy overtook them, but they gave their lives in the service of their fellow men as surely as if they had lost them in some actual rescue operation. Their sacrifice, that of men of experience taking calculated risks in the service of others, would not have been in vain if a greater care and awareness of the dangers of the mountains meant a reduction in the number of calls on the mountain rescue service."

But it was reassuring to people who enjoyed their climbing and fell walking to know that if they did get into difficulties there were people ready to risk their lives to the point of death to bring them succour, said the Archdeacon. The congregation - among the largest at Cockermouth funerals for some time - included representatives of Cockermouth Urban and Rural Councils, police, the education authority, Cockermouth and Keswick Mountain Rescue Teams and other mountaineering organisations, and pupils and staff from Derwent School.

Mr Thomson, who was a bachelor, came to Cockermouth from Gatehouse of Fleet, Scotland, about 20 years ago, when he joined the staff of All Saints' School. He was an experienced mountaineer and had climbed extensively in Great Britain and in the Alps. He took several school parties on climbing holidays, and was founder chairman of Cockermouth Mountaineering Club.

Mr Stephenson, also among the most experienced members of the team, was appointed its secretary at the annual meeting in March.'

The Pepper Pot - Ravenglass

Inscription   None

O.S. Map: English Lakes SW 1:25000   **Grid ref:** 107958

Location

The monument is perched very prominently on a hill above Nether Stainton Farm about 3 miles south of Muncaster Castle on the A595 , but there is no public right of way to it.

Information

It is a magnificent round tower, known locally as the 'Pepper Pot', and has a commanding view over the Esk estuary. Many people believe it was built centuries ago as a monument to the Pennington family of Muncaster Castle, others say it was built by the Penningtons as a hunting shelter. Neither version is correct. The tower is on land owned by the Nicholson family of Nether Stainton and was built by the great-grandfather of Mr John Nicholson, the present owner, as a summer house. Inside, it once had a superbly carved sandstone table and also windows and a door, but over the years vandals have reduced it to an empty wreck. As a result, the Nicholsons refuse to allow public access to the tower and request that people respect their wishes and keep away.

Rawnsley Memorial - Keswick

Inscription

To the honoured memory of Hardwicke Drummond Rawnsley
1851 - 1920

Who greatly loving the fair things of nature and of art Set all his love to the service of God and man. He was Canon of Carlisle, Chaplain to the King. Vicar of Crosthwaite 1883 - 1917 and one of the founders of the National Trust into whose care Friars Crag, Lords Island and a part of Great Wood were given by subscribers who desired that his name should not be forgotten. 7 September 1922

O.S. Map: English Lakes NW 1:25000   **Grid ref:** 264223
Grade: C

Location

The plaque is set into a wall on the left of the path leading from the National Trust's information centre to Friars Crag, on the eastern shore of Derwentwater, Keswick.

Information

Best known as one of the founders of the National Trust, and described by one of his parishioners as 'The most active volcano in Europe', the life story of Canon Hardwicke Drummond Rawnsley could easily fill several volumes. He was born on the 29th of September 1851 at Shiplake, near Henley, where his father was the Vicar, and was one of twins in a family of ten children. He was educated at Uppingham School and Balliol College, Oxford, where he met John Ruskin, (see page 96) who was the Slade Professor of Fine Art, and started a friendship with him that was to last many years. In 1875 Rawnsley worked as a lay preacher in Soho, London, and through Ruskin he met Octavia Hill, (see page 23). Ordained as a minister in 1877, he took the living of Wray on Windermere, and the following year he married Edith Fletcher, of Ambleside. Rawnsley threw himself into his work with such energy and enthusiasm he became ill and had to take six months off work. But soon after arriving home from a tour of the Middle East he was as active as ever and, in 1883, was heavily involved in fighting the proposed Honister to Braithwaite railway, a scheme which, through his efforts, was defeated. He formed the 'Lake District Defence Society' which vigorously contested, and defeated, a proposal to build a railway up Ennerdale; but, once again, overwork drained his health, and in 1890 he became seriously ill and was ordered to take three months holiday. Back home, he devoted his boundless energy to his concern for the countryside and, in 1895, together with Octavia Hill and Sir Robert Hunter, he founded the National Trust for Places of Historic Interest or Natural Beauty. For 26 years, until he died, he was the Trust's honorary secretary.

On Christmas Day 1916, Rawnsley's wife Edith was taken ill after attending a service in Carlisle Cathedral and, before the year had ended, she died. He was so overcome with grief he was unable to attend the funeral service; and after a long convalescence, he announced he could not continue his work without her help and was leaving Crosthwaite. He was deluged with letters pleading with him to stay; but having made up his mind, he retired to Allan Bank, Grasmere, a house in which Wordsworth had lived for three years. Rawnsley was deeply affected by the 1914-18 war and proposed that the men killed should be commemorated in gifts of land. In 1918 he married Eleanor Simpson, a family friend, and they spent their honeymoon touring National Trust properties in Wales and the West country. Early in 1920 he had a mild heart attack. He insisted on keeping an engagement to preach in York, but suffered another heart attack shortly after returning home to Grasmere. Though he seemed to be recovering, he had a relapse and died on the 28th of May. He was buried in Crosthwaite Churchyard beside his first wife, Edith.

Robinson's Cairn - Ennerdale

Inscription

For remembrance of John Wilson Robinson, of Whinfell Hall, in Lorton, who died 1907 at Brigham, one hundred of his comrades and friends raised this. He knew and loved as none other these his native crags and fells, whence he drew simplicity, strength and charm.

> We climb the hill, from end to end.
> In all the landscape underneath
> We find no place that does not breathe
> Some gracious memory of our friend

O.S. Map: English Lakes NW 1:25000   **Grid ref:** 177124

Grade: A

Location

Robinson's Cairn is on the 'High Level' path which runs between Looking Stead, west of the summit of Black Sail Pass, and below the base of Pillar rock to the Ennerdale valley. It is a very popular path, but requires a good head for heights between Robinson's Cairn and Looking Stead. The most direct route to the cairn is from the Ennerdale valley, with spectacular views of Pillar Rock above the forest boundary and from the cairn.

Information

John Wilson Robinson came from a wealthy farming family who owned Whinfell Hall, Lorton, near Cockermouth. Although he carried on the family tradition of farming at Lorton, and was also a popular land agent, he had an intense love for the Lakeland fells and crags and spent all his spare time walking or rock-climbing. He was renowned for his tremendous feats of endurance and his record-breaking walks across the fells but, above all, he was recognised as one of the pioneers of British rock-climbing. His diary records 348 mountain and rock climbs, including Pillar Rock 101 times, Scafell Pinnacle over 50 times and almost 40 ascents of Great Gable. He was the friend and climbing companion of men like Haskett-Smith, who made the first ascent of Napes Needle on Great Gable in 1886, and other noted pioneer climbers of the day. Clad only in tweed suits and hobnailed boots, these early mountaineers made the first ascents of many of the classic rock climbs of the Lake District. John Wilson Robinson was a Vice-President of the Fell and Rock Climbing Club of the English Lake District, and when he died in 1907 at the early age of 55, his friends, mostly members of the club, subscribed to a memorial to him to be placed near Pillar Rock, where he had pioneered so many of the routes.

Despite Robinson's fame and popularity, there was considerable objection to the proposal from some mountaineers on the grounds that it would establish an 'undesirable precedent', but the subscribers to the memorial considered the case an exceptional one and a cairn was built on a knoll on the 'High Level Route' near Pillar Rock during Easter 1908. A bronze plaque, due to be fixed to a rock at the same time, was not ready, and the unveiling ceremony was postponed.

It was planned for June 13th 1908, but the fickle Lakeland weather seemed to be on the side of the objectors and a furious storm broke over Ennerdale, lashing Pillar with gale force winds and torrential rain. Benson Walker, the contractor who had cast the bronze plaque, set off from the Anglers Inn with his men in the early hours of the morning of the 13th, 'and struggled valiantly up the valley then climbed the fell below Pillar Rock pulling the heavy bronze plaque and their tools behind them. They arrived at the cairn just before midday but by the time the Fell and Rock Club members had caught up with them the storm was at its worst and "it was reluctantly decided to curtail the proceedings". The plaque was placed against the rock it was due to be fixed on and while the company huddled together W. Cecil Slingsby, another famous name in Lakeland mountaineering, standing in for W.P. Haskett-Smith who could not attend, gave a glowing speech to the memory of John Wilson Robinson before everyone beat a hasty retreat back to the Anglers Inn and Buttermere.

Describing the scene in a report in the Fell and Rock Club Journal one of the party wrote 'Pillar Rock was almost beyond recognition. The great bastion appeared to be hung with garlands of lace, the well-known gully climbs on the north face being transformed into foaming cataracts. The Liza, which the party intended to cross en route, was in mad impassable spate, and many of its tributary torrents proved too deep and strong to be negotiated. Through blinding sheets of rain, the storm-driven travellers trudged and waded up the bleak valley to the Black Sail footbridge, which at first looked to have been washed away, but ultimately the plank was found several feet under water.'

Two days later Benson Walker and his men returned and fixed the plaque to the rock, and in August a bottle, containing a record of the Memorial written on parchment and encased in a metal box, was buried under the cairn on the summit of Pillar Rock. The total amount subscribed to the Memorial Fund was a little under £41, and the cost of the plaque, plus fixing and expenses, was a touch over £28.

Ross's Camp - Ravenglass

Inscription

Ross's Camp
1883

O.S. Map: English Lakes SW   1:25000   **Grid ref:** 122986
Grade: C

Location

Ross's Camp is on Muncaster Fell, a delightful elongated hill running between Ravenglass and Eskdale Green and easily accessible from either. An enjoyable path winds across the fell to the summit, from where the 360 degree panorama of the coast and the fells is memorable. Ross's Camp is marked on Ordnance Survey maps and is by the side of the path about half a mile on the Eskdale Green side of the summit.

Information

John Ross was the agent for Muncaster Estate during a period around 1883 and lived at The Grove, a large house on the left as you descend into Ravenglass village. The view from Muncaster

Fell was a great favourite of John Ross and his family, and he had a wooden chalet built on the hillock now known as Ross's Camp. A huge granite stone was dug out of the hillside behind Hinning House farm, which can be seen immediately below Ross's Camp in Eskdale. The stone was lifted onto a heavy cart and pulled by a team of horses from Hinning House, along the road past Muncaster Castle, up the track behind Muncaster Chase and by the lovely Muncaster Tarn to its resting place overlooking the Eskdale valley. Here the stone was set on boulders like a table and the inscription chiselled onto it.

Though now only narrow, and at times very boggy, the path over Muncaster Fell was once a well-maintained track capable of taking a coach and horses.

Ruskin Memorial - Keswick

Inscription

(Front)
The first thing which I remember as an event in life was being taken by my nurse to the brow of Friars Crag on Derwentwater

(Back)
The spirit of God is around you, in the air that you breathe. His glory in the light that you see and in the fruitfulness of the earth and the joy of its creatures. He has written for you day by day his revelation and he has granted you day by day your daily bread.

O.S. Map: English Lakes NW 1:25000   **Grid ref:** 263223
Grade: C
Location
Set amongst the trees on Friars Crag on the eastern shore of Derwentwater.

Information

John Ruskin was born in London in February 1819, the same year as Queen Victoria, but socially Ruskin and the future monarch were planets apart. Ruskin's father was a wine merchant, but it did not stop his mother treating her son like royalty. "Were he son to a king," she said, "more care could not be taken of him and every day gives proof of possessing quickness, memory and observation not quite common at his age." But Mrs Ruskin's care for her son went far beyond normal parental concern, and so paranoid was she about the welfare of young John he was never allowed to have toys, to play rough games or have boisterous friends. His formative years were lonely and isolated and so carefully guarded that, when he eventually went up to Oxford, his mother rented accommodation near the college to be with him.

Ruskin began writing poetry when he was only seven, and also showed signs of being an accomplished artist; but his boyhood ambition was to be a geologist and, by the age of fifteen, he was sending articles on geology to magazines. But though his mother dominated his life, she had little control over his natural instincts, and in his youth he fell hopelessly in love with Adèle Domecq, one of the daughters of his father's Spanish business partner. Ruskin was devastated when she married someone else while he was at Oxford, and his health broke down. Suffering from depression and suspected consumption, his parents took him on a long tour of France, Italy and Switzerland. In 1841 the family returned to London but, though young John's health had improved, his heart was still aching. However, when he was introduced to thirteen year old Effie Gray, a distant cousin, he was instantly captivated and wrote a fairy story, 'The King of the Golden River', for her. It was about this time that Ruskin rocked the art world and gained a reputation as an art critic, by staunchly defending the works of the artist Turner and writing and publishing the first volume of his book 'Modern Painters'. He also found time to court Effie Gray and, in 1848 , they were married and set off on a tour of France followed by a year living in Venice.

A generous allowance from his father enabled Ruskin to enjoy a privileged life-style, but he became increasingly conscious of the squalour and poverty in which ordinary people lived. Though his father managed to suppress the publication of several letters destined for the Times describing the social and economic problems of the poor, Ruskin later caused a storm by writing an article for a magazine in which he said:-

'Gentlemen have to learn that it is no part of their duty or privilege to live on other people's toil. They have to learn that there is no degradation in the hardest manual, or the humblest servile, labour when it is honest. But there is degradation in bribery, in indolence, in pride, in taking places they are not fit for, in coining places for which there is no need.'

Surprisingly for a man who had a clear mission to reform society, his personal life was in a mess and, in 1854, his wife Effie had their six year marriage annulled on the grounds of non-consummation and ran off with the artist John Everett Millais.

Ruskin continued writing and lecturing on behalf of the working classes; though, while in Italy in 1858, he experienced an 'Unconversion' which turned him against religion for almost sixteen years. During this time, at the age of 47, he proposed marriage to Rose la Touche, a 17 year old girl he had known since she was a child, but she postponed her decision. Ruskin's father died in 1864 leaving him a considerable fortune, and it enabled him to purchase Brantwood, a large house on the shore of Coniston Water, and also help Octavia Hill with her scheme to buy property in London to house homeless people. He poured thousands of pounds into helping the poor and building museums, and seems to have been a 'soft touch' for anyone looking for a backer for a project; but his fortune could not provide the one thing he sought more than anything else, happiness. In 1872 Rose la Touche, now mentally ill, finally rejected his proposal and three years later she died, completely insane. Perhaps the rejection by Rose sowed the seeds that eventually undermined his own sanity, for he began to have hallucinations which in turn led to recurring mental breakdowns.

In 1887, at the age of 68, he fell in love with Kate Olander, a young art student; and though her parents forbade her to meet Ruskin, they carried on a secret correspondence that might have blossomed had it not been for Ruskin's housekeeper, who intercepted Kate's letters and kept them from him. In 1900, incapacitated and a recluse, John Ruskin, genius and philanthropist, died at Brantwood and was buried in Coniston churchyard.

Ruthwaite Lodge - Patterdale

Inscription

Restored by the maintenance team of Outward Bound Ullswater and dedicated 26.3.93 to the memory of Richard Read and Mike Evans. Tutors from O.B.U. killed on Mount Cook. New Zealand 31.1.88

O.S. Map: English Lakes NE 1:25000   **Grid ref:** 355136
Grade: B

Location

  In a prominent position by the side of the old pack horse route in Grisedale, 2.5 miles west of Patterdale. If approaching from Grasmere, 1 mile east of Grisedale Tarn

Information

  Richard Read was a Senior Instructor at Ullswater Outward Bound Centre in the 1980s. Mike Evans was also an instructor at the Centre during the same period, but left to go to Australia. In 1988 the two friends met up in New Zealand with the intention of climbing Mount Cook, 3,764 metres, the highest peak in New Zealand's South Island; but what exactly happened after they set out for the mountain in January of that year is something of a mystery. Richard told his brother that he and Mike Evans were planning to attempt the climb by a particular route; but, when they were overdue and a search party was formed, they were found dead on a completely different route. Richard's injuries were consistent with a fall, whereas Mike's injuries showed that he had been struck by falling ice. It was assumed that, at some time during the 31st of January, Mike had been swept off the mountain by an avalanche of ice while the pair were roped together, and had pulled Richard off. Richard was age 31 and Mike 25 and, by an odd coincidence they shared the same birth date of March 26th. Richard's ashes were scattered on Birk Crag, close by Outward Bound Ullswater, and Mike's ashes were scattered in Deepdale near Patterdale.

Phil Williamson and Pete Charnley, both Senior Instructors at Ullswater, set up a memorial fund to build a mountain hut in the grounds of Outward Bound Ullswater and raised £18,000; but an architect-designed Scandinavian chalet was turned down by the Lakes National Park Planning Board. Some time later Phil was approached by Matson Ground Estate, owners of much of the Grisedale Valley near Patterdale, who offered to lease Ruthwaite Lodge to the Read Evans Memorial Trust at a peppercorn rent, if they would rebuild and maintain it. The lodge had formerly been leased to Sheffield University, but had been accidentally destroyed by fire by a non-university group who had been given permission to use it.

Phil Williamson and his trustees readily accepted the Matson Ground Estate offer, and much of the debris clearance work and the task of manhandling the massive roof timbers to the site was undertaken by the Windmill Group, a team of youngsters from Blackpool led by Stuart Sykes, a retired community policeman. They were preparing to go out to Africa to help on a building project and the rebuilding of Ruthwaite Lodge was ideal training. With the assistance of Dennis Kitching, a local farmer who took building materials up to the site with his quad bike, and a helicopter which carried up the roof slates, the work was started in spring 1992, and was completed a year later in the spring of 1993.

The opening ceremony was performed on the 26th of March 1993, and again the helicopter helped out by flying Mike's invalid sister and Richard's infirm mother to the site. Steve Howe (O.B.U. Principal at the time) and Mike's father both gave addresses, while Richard's and Mike's mothers jointly unveiled the plaque.

Ruthwaite Lodge is available for use by non-Outward Bound parties at the discretion of the Trustees at Outward Bound Ullswater.

Scafell Pike Memorial - Wasdale

Inscription

In perpetual memory of the men
of the Lake District who fell
for God and King for freedom
peace and right in the Great War
1914 - 1918
This summit of Scafell
was given to the Nation subject
to any Commoners' Rights and placed
in custody of the National Trust
by
Charles Henry Baron Leconfield
1919

O.S. Map: English Lakes SW 1:25000   **Grid ref:** 215073
Grade: A
Location

Built into the summit cairn of Scafell Pike. The most direct route to the summit is from Wasdale by the popular Brown Tongue route and the well-defined path built by the National Trust.

Information

Writing about the indefatigable Canon Rawnsley, one of the founders of the National Trust, in his book 'The National Trust - The First Hundred Years', the author Merlin Waterson says:-

'One of Rawnsley's last but most inspired contributions to the Trust was to propose that the dead should be commemorated in gifts of land. Accordingly in 1920, the year that Rawnsley died, the summit of Scafell Pike was given by the 3rd Lord Leconfield (the future donor of Petworth House in Sussex) as a memorial to the men of the Lake District who had fallen in the Great War.'

Rawnsley was a man who perhaps did more than anyone to focus public attention on the need to care for the countryside, and he was particularly successful in persuading the landed gentry to endow land and property for the benefit of the nation. He would no doubt have been delighted that the men of Lakeland were to be remembered by the gift of England's highest mountain; but, while watching the dedication ceremony from on high, being the outspoken and forthright man he was, he probably longed to bring to the attention of the assembly below that the wording on the plaque was slightly inaccurate as Scafell was a distinct and separate peak half a mile away.

P.D. Boothroyd, in a letter to the magazine 'Cumbria' in July 1962, remembered the dedication ceremony on the 24th of August 1921, when the memorial tablet was built into the summit cairn by men of the Ordnance Survey under the command of a Major:-

'We were staying in Borrowdale and got our information that the event was to take place in two or three days from the Manchester Guardian. I quote from the diary of the above year as follows:-

'With three children cycled to Seathwaite and climbed Scafell Pike by Grain Gill and shoulder of Great End, Building in to Cairn of Memorial tablet. Descended by Piers Gill and Sty Head. Tea at Seathwaite. Grand day with clouds on summit (at intervals).'

The landowner who gave the mountain to the people, Lord Leconfield, or to give him his full title, Charles Henry Wyndham (3rd Baron cr 1859) GCVO, of Cockermouth Castle, Cumberland and of Petworth House, Petworth, Sussex, was born in 1872. He is reputed to have been an eccentric character and a huge eater, big drinker, and an ardent foxhunter. One story about him relates an occasion when the Vicar of a church on one of his estates caught some woodmen preparing to cut down a yew in the churchyard on the orders of His Lordship, and told them to clear off. Word got back to Lord Leconfield who wrote: 'Dear Rector, I shall be obliged if you would not interfere with my servants when they are carrying out my instructions.' The Rector wrote back: 'Thank you for your letter. I shall send round my groom-gardener and my house-parlourmaid to cut down the big cedar tree on your south lawn. I shall be grateful if you will not interfere with my servants when they are carrying out my instructions.'

It was said of Lord Leconfield that he suffered from low blood pressure and the only way he could get his blood to flow properly was to lose his temper!

Scafell Pike is a truly magnificent memorial to the fallen, but it is also a tribute to the generosity of Lord Leconfield and the dedication of Canon Rawnsley.

Seaton Scouts' Memorial - Keswick

Inscription

In Memory of
John Lole
and
Ian Sandelands
1st Seaton Scout Group
1980

O.S. Map: English Lakes NW 1:25000   **Grid ref:** 244274
Grade: B
Location

Approx. 2 miles from Keswick, on the A591 Keswick-Carlisle road, there is a parking area and cafe on the right. From here, a network of paths lead to the top of The Dodd, a conical fell once covered with attractive Spruce, Douglas Fir and Larch; but, for a number of years it has been the victim of a form of arborial euthanasia, officially called landscaping. From the cafe, a well-defined track climbs alongside the gorge of Skill Beck, and emerges onto a forest road. A few metres higher on the right, a stony track leads to another forest road which contours round the fell heading for the summit. Near the top of the road, a narrow muddy path climbs away to the right for the final couple of hundred feet to the summit, where the monument will be found in the shelter of the trees. A breathtaking birds-eye view of Bassenthwaite Lake from the top.

Information

The summit of Dodd Fell has a special significance for members of the 1st Seaton Scout Troop, from Seaton, near Workington. For over forty years, it has been the custom of the Troop, when introducing lads to scouting, to camp for the first time on a site by the edge of Bassenthwaite Lake, and make the summit of Dodd Fell their first fell walk.

The stone was erected on Dodd by the Seaton Scout Troop as a memorial to two young Venture Scouts, John Lole and Ian Sandelands, both 18 years old, who died in accidents within three months of each other during the summer of 1980. John Lole, who was in his first year at University, died rock climbing off Swanage in Dorset, and Ian Sandelands, a police cadet at Penrith, died in a car accident.

Because of the popularity of these two lads, and because they died within 3 months of each other, it was decided to build a monument to their memory and, in the Autumn of 1980, the group spent several weekends ferrying cement, sand and water to the site, and a hole was laboriously dug to sink the stone nearly a metre into the ground to make it stable. The heavy piece of local slate, almost 2 metres long, was hauled to the summit by a team of scouts and friends during frosty weather, when it was very icy and the slate slid easily over the ground.

The tremendous feat was completed and the memorial in situ on New Years Eve 1980.

During Easter 1981 a dedication service, conducted by the Rev. Ian H Bowman, was held at the memorial, and over 40 friends and relatives, including the grandparents of one of the boys, made the long climb to the summit to be present.

Shepherds' Monument - Keswick

Inscription

In Loving Memory of two Skiddaw shepherds
EDWARD HAWELL
of Lonscale
Born Oct. 21st 1815
Died June 2nd 1889
and his son
JOSEPH HAWELL
of Lonscale
Born Dec. 24th 1854
Died Feb. 20th 1891
Noted Breeders of Prize Herdwick Sheep
also to
ROBERT WALKER HAWELL
Born 16th Mar 1851
Died 29th Dec. 1911
Great Shepherd of thy heavenly Flock
These men have left our hill
Their feet were on the living rock
Oh Guide and Bless them still

(on the back)

Also to JOHN HAWELL
Born 2nd July 1848
Died 20th Oct. 1912

O.S. Map: English Lakes NW 1:25000   **Grid ref:** 283257
Grade: C - by car   B - via Latrigg

Location

People in a hurry drive from Keswick, taking the Carlisle road for a short distance until a side road on the right has a sign for Applethwaite and Skiddaw. From Applethwaite, a narrow road climbs steeply to a parking area and the start of the path up Skiddaw by Jenkin Hill. Follow the path until the monument is reached after half a mile of easy walking. Superb views across the Greta valley.

You can avoid the narrow road, and bad-tempered motorists who can't reverse uphill, by walking from Keswick up a path that climbs Latrigg and emerges at the start of the path to Skiddaw. A round trip of about 6 miles, but worth every gasp.

Information

The monument is a memorial to four men of the Hawell family, who farmed at Lonscale, the farm in the valley below the east side of the monument. Edward Hawell was well-known all over the north of England as a breeder of exceptional Herdwick sheep, and regularly won the championship prizes at the prestigious Royal Show and at local shows in Cumberland and Westmorland. According to people who visited the farm, there were four stuffed rams mounted in cases in the hall, and prizes and cards covered the walls in the Herdwick prize room. Local farmers regarded Edward as a great character, and it was said that when he was on his death bed he asked his sons to bring his prize tup up to his bedroom so he could see it for the last time. Terrified at being dragged into the house, the ram put up a tremendous struggle; but, with a pair of well-built sons heaving on its horns and a third hefting his shoulder against its rump, it was bundled up the stairs and into the bedroom and Edward died a happy man.

His son Joseph took over Lonscales and planned to erect a stone monument in memory of his father; but, with the pressure of farm work he never got round to it and, two years later, at the age of 37, he was struck down by a mysterious complaint which affected his face. His doctor lanced a gum but it became infected with erysipelas, a type of gangrene known to country folk as 'St Antony's Fire', and within a month he was dead. The vicar of his Parish was the redoubtable Canon Rawnsley, and, although he was abroad at the time Joseph died, he visited Lonscale on his return. He was told about the idea for a memorial, and shown a letter Joseph had written to a neighbour asking his help to bring a suitable stone down from Lonscale Crag on a sledge. Rawnsley saw to it that a stone was cut from the crag and carved into a cross in memory of the Hawells, and with what he described as "the endless knot their Norse forefathers used, in symbol of eternity" carved above it. He had the names of Edward and Joseph Hawell inscribed on it together, with a verse of his own which begins, 'Great Shepherd of Thy Heavenly Flock'.

Robert Hawell took over the running of the farm and Joseph's widow stayed on as housekeeper. It was said that Joseph's dog, Jess, pined for him for over two months before she could be coaxed back to work on the fell. When Robert eventually gave up the farm and retired to Threlkeld, where he died in 1911, he was the last of the Hawells of Lonscale. John, the elder brother, had left to take a farm in Westmorland and, when he died, it was taken over by his family. In adding the names of Robert and John to the monument, someone has made sure that Edward and his three sons are re-united, and from their lookout on Jenkin Hill can keep a watchful eye on their beloved Herdwicks for all time.

After World War 1, Lonscale farm was acquired by the Spedding family of Mireside, and the grandfather of John Spedding, the present owner of the estate, thought so much of the Hawell family he continued to use the H mark which was daubed on the Hawell sheep to identify them. The 'H' mark is still used on Lonscale sheep to this day.

Simpson's Bridge - Rosthwaite

Inscription

This Bridge was Built
For and at the sole exspence
of Thomas Simpson
May 1851 By Jas Kennedy. Mason

O.S. Map: English Lakes NW 1:2500   **Grid ref:** 261151
Grade: C
Location

The beautifully built local stone bridge is located close to Rosthwaite Post Office, Borrowdale at the start of the track to Watendlath and Stonethwaite.

Information

When the fast-flowing Stonethwaite Beck pours out of the glacial offshoot of the Borrowdale valley that gave it its name, it widens, slows down appreciably and, unless swollen in flood, meanders gently on to join the River Derwent a mile or so below the old-world hamlet of Rosthwaite. As it passes Rosthwaite, the beck flows between the ancient rambling mass of the Royal Oak and Scafell Hotels on the one side, wherein many generations of Borrowdale residents and early travellers have drunk their fill, and the solid, respectable Victorian gentleman's residence of Hazel Bank on the other side.

In the 18th century, John Simpson of Lodore Farm, Borrowdale, married Mary Youdale of Riggside. They had six children; Robert, John, James, William, Dinah and Thomas. Thomas emigrated to America and became a successful New York businessman, while his elder brother John stayed at home and, in 1841, records show that he and his wife Sarah owned and ran the hotels at Rosthwaite, and also farmed 60 acres of land. His brother Thomas, meantime, had made his fortune in America and returned home to Borrowdale and built his dream house on the other side of Stonethwaite Beck, opposite the hotels, and called it Hazel Bank. (It is believed that Hugh Walpole based some of the characters in his Herries novels on the Simpson family and Hazel Bank.) In those days the only means of crossing the beck at Rosthwaite was by a line of stepping stones and in 1851, to enable builders to reach the site of his new house, Thomas engaged a local mason to span the beck with an attractive stone bridge.

What happened to Thomas on a wild February night twenty one years later no-one can be sure. In an era where the reputation of a pillar of the community dictated that newspapers were economical with the truth, the Cumberland Pacquet's report of 'the melancholy death of Thomas Simpson Esq. of Hazel Bank, Rosthwaite, Borrowdale, so long known as one of the leading Borrowdale states-men', discreetly avoided any scandalous innuendo:-

"After spending an evening with a neighbour on Thursday night, he left to go home. Not returning, some anxiety was felt which was intensified by the faithful collie dog coming back without his master and whining uneasily. A search was at once instituted but nothing was seen of the unfortunate gentleman until Friday afternoon when his lifeless body was found half a mile below his house in that part of the river known as Borrowdale beck, opposite the Bowder Stone. The night of Thursday was extremely dark and windy, and it is supposed that Mr Simpson, missing his way, fell or was blown over a low bridge into the stream, being swept away by the impetuous torrent."

Dale's gossip, however, reveals a different story. It appears that Thomas was fond of lively crack and plenty of ale and the neighbour he had been visiting on that fateful night was his brother John, mine host of the Scafell Hotel. Well fortified with Scafell hospitality, Thomas staggered out into the storm, heading for home, and was not seen again until, two days later, his body was pulled out of the beck. Whether he fell over the low parapet of the bridge he had had built in order to reach Hazel Bank, or through an alcoholic haze he saw two bridges and unluckily chose to cross the wrong one, we will never know. But whether or not the unfortunate Thomas met his end through drink, spare him a thought when you pass over his bridge; he has saved thousands of visitors to Borrowdale from getting their feet wet!

The plaque is to be found in the centre of the parapet on the upstream side of the bridge, but to read it you will either have to get a friend to dangle you by the legs over the bridge parapet or stand in the middle of the beck with a pair of binoculars. Have fun!

Slight Side Plane Crash - Eskdale

Inscription

In Memory of P/O Z. Hohne (24)
& Sgt S. Karabin D.F.M. (25)
55 OTU RAF Usworth
Killed on the 12th August 1941
When both their Hurricane Aircraft
struck the mountainside near this point.

This Memorial is dedicated
to both Polish Pilots by
1030 (Whitehaven) SQDN
Air Training Corps during
the 50th Anniversary of the
formation of the A.T.C. and by
The White Eagle Club

O.S. Map: English Lakes SW 1:25000   **Grid ref:** 207051
Grade: A
Location
A most enjoyable path to Slight Side starts opposite Wha House
farm in Eskdale and climbs pleasantly above the Eskdale valley.

Winding through a maze of hillocks, it levels out on a wide expanse of boggy moorland before climbing again towards the craggy face of Slight Side. Before the path leaves the grassy slope and climbs steeply towards the crags, strike diagonally left, heading for Slight Side's left-hand ridge. Odd bits of aircraft, including an engine, will be seen on the way. Nearing the left-hand ridge, keep a look out for a small cross on a cairn and a heap of aircraft wreckage piled near it. Below, in the distance, is Burnmoor Tarn. The monument is not easy to find but is worth the effort.

Information

Although only aged 25, Sergeant Pilot Stanlislaw Karubin of 303 Polish Squadron of the Royal Air Force was a veteran of the "Battle of Britain," in which he flew a Spitfire. He was credited with seven confirmed air victories and awarded a D.F.M. for bravery. Early in 1941, he was posted to 55 OTU at RAF Usworth, near Washington in County Durham, as a flying instructor, teaching pilots to fly Hawker 'Hurricane' fighter planes.

Pilot Officer Zygmunt Hohne was a year younger at 24, but had also seen active service with the Polish Air Force and was one of many Polish pilots to be posted to RAF Usworth on the Hurricane conversion course.

On the morning of the 12th of August 1941, Sergeant Karubin took off from RAF Usworth in Hurricane V for Victor 7742, closely followed by Pilot Officer Hohne in Hurricane V for Victor 6565. They were on a training flight which was to take them almost due west to Silloth, then down the coast for a few miles before turning east and heading back to Usworth. Weather forecasting was not as efficient as it is now and, although it was midsummer, the two aircraft soon flew into thick cloud over the Cumberland coast. According to an official report, 'the leader was unaware of his position'. Perhaps thinking they were still over the sea, and hoping for a glimpse of the coast to establish their position, the two pilots put their aircraft into a dive to get below the cloud but, tragically, they had strayed miles off course and were over the Lakeland fells. Diving through the cloud, they crashed simultaneously into Horn Crag on Slight Side, above Eskdale. Both pilots died instantly, and the heap of wreckage is a grim reminder of how two young lives were lost in the cause of peace.

Tennyson's Monument - Keswick

Inscription

> Then quickly rose Sir Bedivere, and ran,
> And, leaping down the ridges lightly, plunged
> Among the bulrush-beds, and clutch'd the sword,
> And strongly wheel'd and threw it. The great brand
> Made lightenings in the splendour of the moor,
> And flashing round and round, and whirled in an arch,
> Shot like a streamer of the northern morn,
> Seen where the moving isles of winter shock
> By night with noises of the northern sea.
> So flash'd and fell the brand Excalibur:
> But ere he dipt the surface, rose an arm
> Clothed in white samite, mystic, wonderful,
> And caught him by the hilt, and brandished him
> Three times, and drew him under the meer.
> Alfred, Lord Tennyson   Morte d'Arthur II 133-146
> This lectern commemorates the visit to
> this place of the Tennyson Society 18th May 1974

O.S. Map: English Lakes NW 1:25000   **Grid ref:** 226285
Grade: C
Location
  On north shore of Bassenthwaite Lake - Catstock Wood - Mireside Estate

Information

The brothers James and Edward Spedding of Mirehouse estate, near Keswick, had a long association with the poet Tennyson and, perhaps better than most, would have been aware of his unhappy childhood which, in his youth and later life, was often reflected in the gloomy and depressive nature of his personality and his poetry. Alfred Tennyson was born on the 5th of August 1809, one of 12 children, 8 boys and 4 girls, of George Tennyson, a violent and alcoholic Lincolnshire vicar. Given the circumstances in which they lived it is hardly surprising that one of Alfred's brothers was insane, another mentally ill, a third an opium addict, a fourth an alcoholic, and the rest of the family each succumbed to a mental breakdown during their lifetime.

Distraught at the death of one of his closest friends at Cambridge, Tennyson stayed with the Speddings for several weeks in the spring of 1835, taking a stagecoach from London to Kendal, then a five hour coach journey to Keswick. In the evenings, it was the custom at Mirehouse to have a 'serious tea', with 'many varieties of cakes, with divers jams and marmalades, and this was the great time for talk.' James Spedding sketched Tennyson 'sitting reading, wrapped in his cloak.' It is widely believed that his stay at Mirehouse, close to the edge of Bassenthwaite Lake, gave the poet much of his inspiration for his long poem 'Morte d'Arthur'.

At the age of 27 he fell in love with Emily Sellwood, a bridesmaid at the wedding of his brother Charles, but they had an unhappy courtship and he was 42 before he finally plucked up courage to 'take the plunge.' On the 13th of June, 1850 , they were married near Henley by Drummond Rawnsley, the father of the renowned Canon Rawnsley who was to found the National Trust. They spent their honeymoon in a house in the grounds of Monk Coniston, during which time Alfred climbed Coniston Old Man with the writer Coventry Patmore. He took Emily boating on Coniston Water, and by coach to Rydal to look at Wordsworth's house, 'but did not go in.' An entry in the Rydal Mount visitors' book for May 1835 suggests that Tennyson was taken to meet Wordsworth by James Spedding while he was a guest at Mirehouse, but the two great literary figures do not appear to have had much regard for each other's work. Tennyson described Wordsworth's poetry as 'thickancled', though, when asked what he thought of Tennyson's poetry, Wordsworth was rather more diplomatic and replied that perhaps his lack of admiration came from his own inability to accommodate himself to a new style of beauty. However, by the spring of 1845 they had become friends and, having had two of Tennyson's poems read to him by a friend, Wordsworth said graciously, though perhaps still with a hint of reservation, "I must acknowledge that those two poems are very solid and noble in thought. Their diction also seems singularly stately."

Like Wordsworth, Tennyson was granted a pension from the Civil List to relieve him from poverty; but, unlike Wordsworth he eventually made a lot of money from his fame as a poet and lived in splendour, moving between his large houses on the Isle of Wight and in Sussex. He was a personal friend of Queen Victoria and Prince Albert and, when Wordsworth died in April 1850, the Prince wrote to Tennyson inviting him to become Poet Laureate. In 1883, he took the final step up to the pinnacle of fame when he became Baron Tennyson of Aldworth and Freshwater

Alfred Lord Tennyson died at the age of 83 on the 6th of October, 1892 , at Aldworth, his home in Sussex, named in honour of the village from which the ancestors of his wife Emily had originated. With much pomp and ceremony he was buried in Westminster Abbey, but none of the Royal Family attended his funeral. Neither did more than a handful of his friends, who during his life had included Dickens, Ruskin, Arnold and a host of other eminent literary and political names. Many had become so disenchanted with his aggressive and objectionable behaviour, blamed on his family history of mental illness, they had turned their backs on him.

In an orgy of well-intentioned but regrettable vandalism, his son Hallam Tennyson, sorted out 40,000 letters and destroyed three-quarters of them, including almost all the letters his father had written to Emily before their marriage. By a stroke of fortune, the earliest wax cylinder recordings made by Thomas Edison were of Tennyson reading some of his poems, and they have survived.

The memory of the time Tennyson spent in the Lake District lives on in his connections with the Speddings of Mirehouse, and in the readings of his poems performed in the open air 'theatre' close to the Tennyson monument.

Tom Wren's Boulder - Ennerdale

Inscription

In Memory of
TOM WREN
1913-1998

O.S. Map: English Lakes NW 1:25000   **Grid ref:** 7191219
Grade: C

Location

Attached to a large glacial boulder, known as Tom Wren's Boulder, by the edge of the forest road on the south side of the river Liza, a short distance upstream from the Fell and Rock Bridge in the Ennerdale valley.

Information

When the Forestry Commission acquired the Ennerdale valley in 1925 and built two workers' bungalows at Gillerthwaite, the first tenants were John Wren and his wife Nellie. Several of their sons also worked in the forest but one by one they left home for other occupations. In 1927, at the age of 14, Tom Wren gave up working on a local farm to join his father who by now had been appointed foreman in charge of the forest workers.

A programme of fencing the entire forest boundary was in full swing, and a series of paths had been built by the men to enable a mule, owned by Tom's father, to carry the heavy bundles of fence posts and rolls of netting up the fellside. Tom's first job when he reported for work on Monday the 16th of November 1927 was helping to load the mule and, in places below Pillar Rock where it was too rough for the animal to negotiate, he had to carry the posts and rolls of netting on his back.

When the boundary fence was completed, the boggy hillside had to be drained and young Tom and his companions spent months digging ditches and diverting water courses before planting could be started. The working conditions of the men in those days was particularly arduous. There was no free issue of waterproof clothing, and if they could not work because of bad weather they did not get paid. When King George V died in 1936 the men were given the day off for the funeral, but were told that if it rained on the day they could not have worked so they would not get paid. Fortunately the sun shone for the funeral and they got their pay! Tom and three others were not so lucky when, on another occasion, while planting trees near Pillar Rock they were asked to assist in a mountain rescue. They spent hours helping to carry the body of a climber over Black Sail Pass to Wasdale, but their public-spirited action cost them a severe reprimand and a day's pay for leaving their job without permission.

While working below Pillar, the only shelter the men had from the rain, snow and gales was an old tarpaulin they tied to one end of a large glacial boulder and crouched under. Determined to find something better, Tom managed to acquire an old hen hut which, having been transported up the valley after working hours and fixed against the boulder, provided 'luxury' shelter for a number of years.

In spite of the hardships he experienced working in the forest and living in an extremely isolated location, Tom Wren considered the Ennerdale valley to be the most beautiful place on earth, and when he died in February 1998 the large boulder was named in his memory.

Two Walks Monument - Thirlmere

Inscription

A record of two walks from here
over the Armboth Fells
July 1833 - 43
which inspired Matthew Arnold's poem
'Resignation'
And in reverent memory of the poet
Born 24 Dec 1822
Died 15 April 1888

We left just ten years since you say,
That way-side inn we left to-day

And now in front behold outspread
Those upper regions we must tread
Mild hollows, and clear heathy swells
The cheerful silence of the fells
MA

O.S. Map: English Lakes NW 1:25000   **Grid ref:** 325137
Grade: C
Location
The monument stone is easily found close to the telephone box beside Wythburn Church on the A591 Grasmere-Keswick road where it runs along the side of Thirlmere.
Information
Hartley Coleridge once said of the Arnolds, father and son, that they 'were suckled on Latin and weaned upon Greek', but it is clear that they also had an appetite for the Lake District. Matthew Arnold, the poet, seems to have been keen on long-distance walks, and the stone at Wythburn commemorates two marathon walking sessions, first in July 1833, then ten years later in 1843. Born in Laleham, near Windsor, Matthew was the second child, and eldest son, of the eleven children of Dr Thomas Arnold, who was appointed Headmaster of Rugby School in 1828. The Arnolds spent a lot of time in the Rydal-Ambleside area and once rented the superb Brathay Hall at Clappersgate - now an Outdoor Centre. Thomas Arnold was a close friend of William Wordsworth and he went on regular walks with him. "We had a good fight about the Reform bill during a walk up Greenhead Ghyll...but I am sure that our political disagreement did not interfere with our enjoyment of each other's society." In a letter to a friend in 1832 Thomas Arnold wrote, "We are thinking of buying or renting a place at Grasmere or Rydal......for not only are the Wordsworths and the scenery a great attraction......I got acquainted with the poorer people besides, and you cannot tell what a home-like feeling all of us entertain towards the valley of the Rotha." Looking ahead to building a house for his retirement from Rugby School, it was the "shrewd knowledge and advice of Wordsworth", and the poet's offer to "facilitate the purchase as far as is in my power", that enabled Thomas Arnold to buy 20 acres of land at Fox How, on the old coach road that follows the River Rothay from Rydal to Rothay Bridge near Ambleside.

Fox How was ideally placed for exploring the Lake District, but the Arnolds appear to have preferred to start their long walks to the Cumberland coast from the Nags Head Inn at Wythburn by Thirlmere, (now demolished.) It was from there, in July 1833, that eleven year old Matthew set out with his elder sister Jane - known as "K" to the family - his father, and Capt. Hamilton, a friend of his father, and walked by way of Watendlath, 'the town, the highway and the plain', and :-

'.....as the balmy darkness fell
We bathed our hands with speechless glee,
That night, in the wide-glimmering sea.'

Ten years later Matthew repeated the walk again, this time in the company of his sister Jane, now Mrs W.E. Forster:-

'The self-same shadows now, as then,
Play through this grassy upland glen;
The loose dark stones on the green way
Lie strewn, it seems, where then they lay;
These are not changed; and we, you say,
Are scarce more changed, in truth, than they.

The above quotations are from Arnold's lengthy poem about the walk which he called 'Resignation' and dedicated to 'Fausta', believed to be his pet name for his sister Jane. The poem is almost as long as the walk itself, but unfortunately it gives few clues as to the exact route. On both occasions they went over Wythburn Fells to Keswick, but whether from there they went by way of Cockermouth to the coast at Workington or through Borrowdale, Buttermere, and Loweswater to Whitehaven is not revealed.

It is ironic that Matthew Arnold, a man who delighted in arduous long-distance walks, should die of a heart attack while running to catch a tram in Liverpool in 1888. He was 66.

Like so many of the Lake District monuments to great literary figures and outstanding events, the Two Walks stone was set up by Canon Rawnsley.

William Porter's Monument - Wasdale

Inscription

William Curwen Porter
Master Eskdale and
Ennerdale Foxhounds
Fell here Salvers Hunt 1st Nov 1952
Died 2nd Nov 1952

He's away my lads away

Note: Salvers Hunt was usually held during the time when shepherds were salving their sheep i.e. smearing the fleece with a mixture of tar and rancid butter to keep the wool waterproof through the winter.

O.S. Map: English Lakes SW 1:25000   **Grid ref:** 151057
Grade: C
Location
   Making for Wasdale Head, the approach roads from Gosforth and Santon Bridge meet at a junction close to the shore of Wastwater. A short distance from the junction, travelling towards Wasdale

Head, the small stone monument will be seen on the top of a hillock.

Information

The West Cumberland Times for the 12th of November, 1952, devoted an unusual amount of space to the passing on of a legend in the dales of West Cumbria when the hunting correspondent wrote:-

"A stranger visiting Eskdale last Wednesday might well have wondered at the unprecedented traffic which crowded the narrow and tortuous roads of Eskdale valley. Where did they all come from? The answer would have been: From all parts of the North of England. These men had travelled long distances to pay a tribute of deep respect to one of the greatest hunters of all times, Willie Porter, Master of the Eskdale and Ennerdale Foxhounds.

The church failed completely to accommodate all who sought admission. Indeed there were three or four times as many outside the church as inside. It was very fitting that the remains of this gallant hunter should be carried to their last resting place by men steeped in foxhunting on the fells. They were Willie Irving, late huntsman of the Melbreak, Arthur Irving, present huntsman of the Eskdale and Ennerdale, Tyson Irving and Harry Irving, the noted Bootle wrestlers, Wilson and Stephen Knowles, and T. Cowman of Fieldhead.

Like most things, the Eskdale pack of foxhounds started from small beginnings. In days of long ago a man of small stature arrived in the valley accompanied by a poaching dog. This was none other than 'La'al' Tommy Dobson, who will go down in history as one of the most successful of Fell foxhunters. At that time he earned his daily bread as a bobbin turner and lived with the Porter family. Eventually he added a hound or two to his poaching dog. More hounds were added and young Porter, already deeply interested in hunting, became, under the able tuition of 'La'al' Tommy, an expert hunter, so much so in fact that Tommy declared that 'Port' (as he called him) was his superior.

Tommy lived and died with the Porter family and he left the legacy of hounds to Willie Porter, and from 1910 the subject of this note acted as huntsman. There may have been equals but never a superior amongst fell foxhunters. He had a wonderful command over hounds, and over men, for that matter too. He was not master in name only, his word in the hunting field was law and there may be some who will remember the "ticking off" they received when they had transgressed, wittingly or otherwise, the laws of hunting. Willie Porter had a wonderful hunting voice, clear and penetrating as the proverbial bell. Porter was a stickler for time and was never known to be late. Hunting from the Anglers Inn, Ennerdale, he was asked to wait for a well-known hunter. Pulling out his watch he said, "No, it is nine o'clock and I would not wait for the King of England," and so the hounds moved off.

In addition to hunting he was an outstanding farmer and had more than a local reputation as a breeder and exhibitor of Herdwick sheep. When he had to curtail his hunting activities owing to increasing years he maintained his interest by breeding hounds and doing the major portion of the kennel work and was engaged in this work right up to the time of his death. Mr Porter had broadcast frequently in feature programmes about the Lake District and hunting.

Keeping faith with tradition, he took the pack up to Wasdale Head on Saturday to give the dalesmen an outing and, in spite of not having enjoyed good health for some time, Mr Porter decided that he would participate too. As hounds went off up Middle Fell, he was following with friends when suddenly he collapsed and fell headlong into swampy ground. He was quickly rescued and accompanied back to the starting point, and was taken back home by car and immediately put to bed. Mr Porter subsequently lapsed into a coma from which he did not rally."